DARK DREAMS:

The Story of

STEPHEN
KING

DARK DREAMS:
The Story of
STEPHEN
KING

Nancy Whitelaw

MORGAN
REYNOLDS
PUBLISHING
Greensboro, North Carolina

WORLD WRITERS

CHARLES DICKENS
JANE AUSTEN
STEPHEN KING
RALPH ELLISON
ROBERT FROST

DARK DREAMS: THE STORY OF STEPHEN KING

Copyright © 2006 by Nancy Whitelaw

To Bob and Dee Keller
with endless admiration for the lives you lead
and many thanks for all your help

Library of Congress Cataloging-in-Publication Data

Whitelaw, Nancy.
    Dark dreams : the story of Stephen King / Nancy Whitelaw.— 1st ed.
        p. cm.
Includes bibliographical references and index.
    ISBN-13: 978-1-931798-77-8 (lib. bdg.)
    ISBN-10: 1-931798-77-X (lib. bdg.)
    1. King, Stephen, 1947- 2. Novelists, American—20th century—
Biography. 3. Horror tales—Authorship. I. Title.
    PS3561.I483Z915 2006
    813'.54—dc22

                            2005020112

Printed in the United States of America
First Edition

CONTENTS

ONE

Learning Fear

Ever the storyteller, Stephen King claims that the last words his family ever heard from his father were "I'm going to go out and get a pack of cigarettes"—an expression straight out of a hard-luck potboiler.

The future writer's father, Donald E. King, married Nellie Ruth Pillsbury shortly before the United States entered World War II. After serving in the Merchant Marine, he returned home with hopes and dreams. On September 14, 1945, the couple adopted a son, David. On September 21, 1947, Ruth gave birth to another son, Stephen Edwin King, in Portland, Maine. When Stevie King was two, his father walked out of their lives forever. Those were scary times.

Opposite: *Stephen King.* (Courtesy of AP Photos.)

The family moved frequently as Ruth went from job to job: store clerk, presser in a laundry, doughnut maker in a bakery—any work that would bring in money. Besides Maine, they logged time in Massachusetts, Chicago, and Wisconsin, often staying with or near Ruth's siblings and relatives. For Dave and Stevie it was a life of making friends and then moving away, finding new fields to play in and then moving away, making friends and then moving again.

The brothers became best friends. When Ruth had to work and could not afford a sitter, the boys took care of themselves. From the time Dave could read, Ruth told him to keep Stevie entertained with stories. Their favorites were comic books with bright pictures, tales full of action, suspense, and strong heroes. As soon as Stevie could read, they took turns reading to each other. The books helped the boys escape the loneliness of an empty house and the bleakness of their day-to-day survival.

Stephen King's earliest memory is one of imagination. He was about three years old and pretending to be a strongman in the Ringling Brothers Circus spotlight. He could hear the applause as he lifted a heavy cinder block, unaware that its insides were filled with wasps. When he bowed to acknowledge the make-believe crowd, a wasp flew out of the cinder block and stung him. He dropped the cinder block on his foot.

Stevie watched his mother leave the house early every day, either to work or to look for a job. Most nights she was exhausted when she arrived home. The next

Ruth King with her sons, David and Stevie (center). (Independent Picture Services)

morning, tired or not, she was back out in the world, earning money for her family. Looking back on his early life, Stephen King credits his mother with teaching him the importance of hard work and the need for perseverance.

It didn't matter how tired she was when she got back home from work—Ruth checked on what the boys had been doing by asking them to tell her what they had read. Then she took her turn reading aloud to her sons, sometimes comic books and sometimes her favorite adventure stories, such as Robert Louis Stevenson's *Treasure Island.*

These stories fueled a mind that became increasingly inquisitive. When he was five or six, Stevie asked his mother if she had ever seen a dead person. She told him a story about a young girl who got caught in an undertow on a beach. The girl screamed for help but no rescue boat could reach her in time. His mother could only hear the screams and could not see the girl, so then Stevie wanted to know if his mother had ever seen anyone die. She told him about watching a sailor jump off the roof of a hotel: "He splattered. The stuff that came out of him was green." Ruth trusted her son's ability to handle hard reality. Stevie stored those images away in his memory.

Like most children, Stevie had his fears. He was afraid of spiders, the number thirteen, sewers, and the dark. He told his mother he had to be able to see in order to go to sleep. Sympathetic, she gave him a night-light. One night, after he snuck downstairs to listen to a radio program that his mother had said was too scary for him, the tiny light was no longer enough. The program was a radio adaptation of Ray Bradbury's *Mars Is Heaven,* a story of space travelers who journey into a night of terror. Stevie listened to descriptions of faces dripping, noses turning into trunks, mouths becoming gaping caverns, and cheeks turning yellow. "I didn't sleep in my bed that night," he recalled. "I slept in the doorway where the real and rational light of the bathroom bulb could shine on my face."

He has a terrifying memory of pain from when he was six years old. It started with a visit to a doctor for an earache. The doctor smiled and said, "Relax, Stevie, this won't hurt." Then he punctured the child's eardrum to let out an infection. Stevie felt a pain so strong that he was breathless for a moment before he began to scream. Unfortunately, the doctor had to perform the procedure on three additional occasions, each time beginning with the same five words: "Relax, Stevie, this won't hurt." Later, King said any doctor who told such a lie "should be jailed immediately, time of incarceration to be doubled when the lie is told to a child." He said, "I think that in some deep valley of my head, that last scream is still echoing."

Between his ear problems and bouts with strep throat, Stevie missed so much of first grade that school administrators required him to stay home for the rest of the year before beginning first grade again in the fall. During that time, he consumed a steady diet of science fiction and horror comic books—about six tons of comics, he has said. In the comic books, heroes like Terry and the

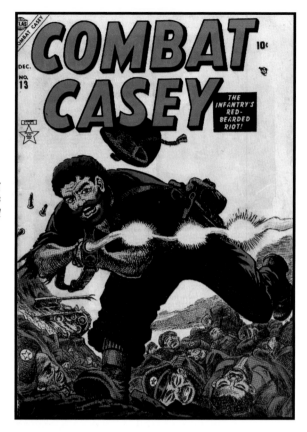

Comic books provided young Stevie King with some of his earliest exposure to horror and science fiction stories.

Pirates, Captain Video, and Combat Casey destroyed enemy weapons while declaring their intentions to fight evil.

His earliest inclination toward writing came when he began copying these comics, sometimes word for word, other times adding his own descriptions of scenes. His mother thrilled Stevie by praising his additions. She told him she was sure he could write better material than what he was reading and suggested he write a comic book of his own. His mother liked four of his original stories so much that she sent them to relatives. She also paid him twenty-five cents for each one. Stephen King had become a professional writer.

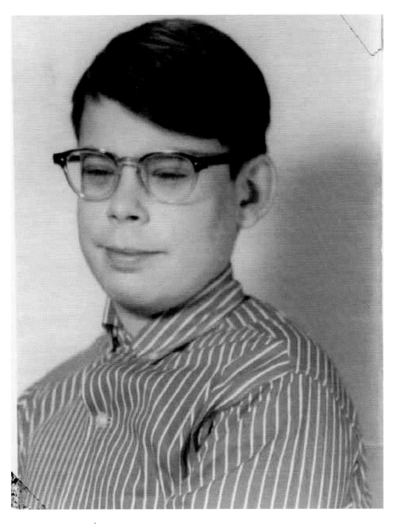

A school picture from Stevie King's grade-school years.

His mother constantly pushed Stevie and his brother to establish goals and to excel in school. She continued to read to the boys whenever they asked, although she commonly worked fifty hours a week. She also read a lot herself, calling her books "cheap vacations." Sometimes all three of the Kings read paperbacks as they ate supper. When Stevie was just seven years old, he saw his mother reading Robert Louis Stevenson's *Dr. Jekyll and Mr. Hyde,* a classic story of good versus evil about a respectable society man who changes into a murderous villain at nightfall with the consumption of a special potion. When Stevie asked her to read it to him, she hesitated because she thought it might be too frightening. Then she decided that she would pass her love of scary books on to her children.

The King family moved to Stratford, Connecticut, for the start of Stevie's second-grade year. They would remain there for four years, their longest stay in any one community to that point. About this time, Stevie started attending Methodist church and Sunday school regularly. Like most children, Stevie found the idea of God both fascinating and puzzling. He heard exciting, sometimes terrifying stories of God's rewards and punishments. In one story, a man named Jonah was thrown off a ship and swallowed by a whale in punishment for turning away from God. Another story told of Adam and Eve's son Cain, who had not shown the proper respect for God's commandments. In retaliation, God cursed all Cain's descendants. In another story, God sent a great 150-day flood to drown all men on earth who disobeyed God's commands. This flood destroyed all men except Noah, God's only faithful servant. One vivid New Testament story of horror was the death of Jesus, who was tortured, forced to wear a crown of thorns, and nailed to a cross.

The stories that Stevie heard stayed in his mind. Sometimes they came back to him as dreams. He would always remember a dream he had when he was about eight years old. In the dream, he saw a hanged man dangling from a scaffold. As the body swung in the breeze, Stevie saw that the face had been pecked by birds. Then he saw that the face on the body was his own. He remembered this dream when he wrote *'Salem's Lot* nearly twenty years later.

Dreams were not the only things Stephen King stored on his mental hard drive. He filed away the image of the mother of a girl in his class who obsessed over religion. A weedy neighborhood area bisected with train tracks held special fascination for him. He and his brother spent hours exploring this place, which they called a jungle, until tragedy struck. One of the boys they were playing with was run over by a freight train while either playing on or crossing the tracks. Another memory etched in King's mind was of watching the body of a victim of a boating accident being pulled from a local pond. In keeping with the writer's dictum that one should write what one knows, Stephen King kept these horrifying experiences fresh in his head.

As an adult, King doesn't find it strange that children accept fantasy and horror. After all, he says, they are encouraged to accept Santa Claus, the Easter Bunny, and fairy tales without question. The stories they hear in Sunday school are about devastating floods, famines, deadly jealousy, and murder. Sometimes, childhood fears remain through adulthood. King says he wrote his block-buster *It* to pursue fears from his own childhood. Often considered his best work, *It* interweaves themes of child abuse, good and evil, and trust and love with scenes of relentless horror.

The Kings didn't get their first television until 1958, slightly behind many people in the country. As a result, Steve developed a love for moving pictures at the movie theater. He and David went to the horror movies as often as they could. His first movie, and one of his favorites, was *Creature from the Black Lagoon*. It featured a scaly monster in the Amazon River who barricaded the mouth of a stream to trap the anthropologists who worked there. Steve knew that the "monster" in the movies was really just an actor wearing a monster suit. He could even see glimpses of the zipper up the back. Still, that monster, that thing, that creature, became a presence in Steve's life. He lived in Steve's closet and in the upstairs hall, and in his life, just waiting to pounce. Besides terrifying him, it made him want to create his own stories so he could terrify others: "I wanna do that! I'm really scared. I want to make other people as scared as I am."

Another science fiction movie that made a lasting impression was *Earth vs. the Flying Saucers,* which Steve saw when he was ten years old. In the final reel of the film, the kids watched aliens attack Washington, D.C., in flying saucers. Suddenly the screen went blank. The theater manager appeared in front of the screen and, in a trembling voice, told the audience that the Russians had just put a satellite, Sputnik, into orbit around the Earth. It's unlikely that many of the children in the crowd could grasp the true importance of such a development. More likely, they were disappointed by the interruption of the on-screen action. They were too young to know their country was in the middle of a new kind of war: the Cold War.

The Cold War began with the end of World War II. The United States and the Union of Soviet Socialist Republics (USSR), two of the triumphant Allied powers, competed for strategic positioning and influence in Eastern Europe and Asia. The U.S. believed that a democratic capitalist government was best; the USSR believed in communism. The U.S. supported other countries that embraced democracy while the USSR supported those that adopted communism. This opposition came to a boil with the Korean War, which started in 1950. The U.S. supported democratic South Korea while the USSR supported Communist North Korea.

As tensions increased, so did military buildup, especially of nuclear weaponry. The Cold War was so named because no weapons were actually used, although there were many confrontations. Included in the "battle plans" of each country were spying, propaganda, a race to build up nuclear arms, and a desire to be first in space exploration. Civil defense drills were held all over America. People were encouraged to build bomb shelters using plans published in a government pamphlet entitled *You Can Survive*. Schools insisted on regular "bomb drills"

During the Cold War years of the 1950s, students across the country learned to prepare for the possible doom of nuclear war by practicing bombing drills such as this one, known as "duck and tuck." (Courtesy of AP Photos.)

in which students were taught to duck under their desks during simulated bombing attacks.

The constant threat of danger, even of annihilation, led to the spread of fear throughout the United States. The news of Russia's triumph in the space race spurred hysteria across the country. And while Steve King and the other kids couldn't know all the implications of a single Russian satellite, they could certainly feel fear. And fear made Steve King feel alive.

TWO

Writer Rebel

I n 1958, when Steve was eleven years old, his family
settled in Durham, Maine, a town of about a thousand people. After years of seeing Ruth move from one
low-paying job to the next, her siblings arranged for her
to take care of their ailing parents, both in their eighties,
in exchange for room and board. The Kings had no
indoor plumbing, got their water from a well, and took
baths at an aunt's house about a half mile away. When
the family well went dry, the brothers lugged water
from the town pump in steel milk cans. For Steve, the
most thrilling thing about their new home was that it
was close to his mother's sister, Aunt Ethelyn, and her
husband, Uncle Clayt. Ethelyn and Clayt's farm no
longer housed animals, but it did hold items fascinating to a boy, like chicken skeletons, which Steve

believed held secrets in the black sockets where eyes had once been.

As he would all his life, Steve picked up ideas for stories from everything he read, from whatever he saw on the screen, and from people he met. Uncle Clayt amazed Steve, partly because of the endless stories he told and partly because he was a dowser—one who promised to find water anywhere using a special wishbone-shaped dowsing rod (or divining rod) made from the branch of an apple tree. Steve could not see any logic in dowsing but followed his uncle around as he searched for water. Steve saw the rod twist in his uncle's hands and point toward the ground. Then Uncle Clayt let him hold the rod, and Steve felt it jerk almost out of his hands, as if there was a mysterious force beneath the surface. The well-drillers found an abundance of water just one hundred feet below the surface at the very spot to which Uncle Clayt had led them.

In Aunt Ethelyn's musty old attic, Steve encountered his first serious fantasy-horror fiction in *The Lurking Fear and Other Stories,* written by early-twentieth-century author H. P. Lovecraft. As he read the stories, Steve had that "dowser feeling" again, the flash of discovery he had experienced when the applewood branch turned over in his hands and pointed down. He says his interior dowsing rod reacted to Lovecraft's writing. He devoured the tales of ghouls, psychic possession, unspeakable evil, and mythical worlds in which time and space were dislocated.

H. P. LOVECRAFT

H. P. Lovecraft.

Howard Phillips Lovecraft lived a brief forty-six years, dying in 1937. His love of both writing and science developed before he was ten. As a boy, he frequently suffered from illnesses, many of them psychological, and was forced to do much of his learning on his own. He suffered a nervous breakdown in his final high school year, failing to gain his diploma or admission to Brown University, in his hometown. Lovecraft adopted the ways of a hermit, cutting himself off from society and devoting himself to writing poetry and essays.

When he emerged five years later, he began writing fiction again, as he had in high school. He wrote novels, novellas, and dozens of stories published in a variety of magazines. He also wrote literary criticism and essays. Today, the best of his fiction is collected in scholarly volumes and studied by literary critics worldwide. His influence has been felt by the famous, including King and Joyce Carol Oates, and by the novice writer trying to find footing in the world of horror.

Without much thought, he had assumed that the movies were fantasy; he believed that Lovecraft's stories were real. What made the stories especially real for Steve was that they were set in New England. He imagined that the community and area where the Kings lived could be a perfect setting for horror stories. He could not put the books down, even after Aunt Ethelyn said she disapproved of his reading them. But within a couple of weeks, the books disappeared. He never found out who took them.

Lovecraft's wasn't the only writing Steve found in the attic. He also uncovered boxes and boxes of mysteries, science fiction, and horror novels that had belonged to Donald King, who had used those books as inspiration for his own writing. While none of the elder King's stories had ever been accepted for publication, he had received some encouraging rejections. Steve's mother said that her husband lacked persistence. She said he might have sold his work if he had tried harder—just as he might have saved their marriage if he had tried harder.

Steve read other genres besides the horror and fantasy that appealed so greatly to him. He remembered waiting for the weekly mail delivery of the *Saturday Evening Post*, a magazine famous for the short stories it featured: "I'd meet [the postman] at the end of the walk, dancing from one foot to the other as if I badly needed to go to the bathroom, my heart in my throat. Grinning rather cruelly, he'd hand me an

THE SATURDAY EVENING POST

An Illustrated Weekly
Founded A.D. 1728 by Benj. Franklin

MAY 20, 1916   5c. THE COPY

Norman Rockwell

THE EMPIRE BUILDERS—By Mary Roberts Rinehart

Steve King was not alone in his passion for the Saturday Evening Post. *The magazine was immensely popular throughout America for its high-quality mainstream fiction by such literary greats as John Steinbeck and Ray Bradbury, as well as its art. American painter Norman Rockwell did illustrations and covers for the magazine from 1916 to 1963. The* Post's *popularity only began to dwindle once the television became a common installment in most households.*

electric bill. Nothing but that. Finally he relents and gives me the *Post* . . . stories. Long ones, short ones, and the last chapter of the serial. Praise God!"

When he was twelve years old, Steve found a good friend in Christopher Chesley. Both boys loved books and movies. Like Steve, Chris wanted to be writer, and they shared dreams about their futures. Chris and Steve gravitated toward stories with fear at their base. They read favorites aloud to each other, especially horror stories. Soon, they were writing stories together—Steve writing one paragraph, Chris the next, and back to Steve for the third. But Steve didn't need a partner to pursue his new passion. He spent hours at home with his old typewriter, trying to make his fingers keep up with his ideas. The missing *n* key on his typewriter did not bother him. After he took the paper out of the typewriter, he pencilled in an *n* in each space left by the missing key.

When Steve was twelve years old, he and brother Dave produced a series of newsletters titled *Dave's Rag* and signed up twenty neighbors to subscribe to it for a dollar each. Using the old typewriter and a mimeograph machine Dave maintained, they put together a newsletter that included bits of information about residents of their town: somebody's recovery from surgery, names of guest speakers at a local church, recent visitors, and jokes. Some issues contained an advertisement for a story by Steve titled "Land of 1,000,000 Years Ago" about twenty-one prisoners on an island. The price of the story was thirty cents. Another ad promoted the sale of a condensed anthology of thirty-one classics, including *Kidnapped* and *The Adventures of Tom Sawyer.* A copy of *Dave's Rag,* with the filled-in n's, appears in the front matter of King's book *On Writing.*

After seeing a film version of Edgar Allan Poe's "The Pit and the Pendulum," Steve wrote his own version of the story. He'd already been using the mimeograph to run off the stories he wrote and felt this one could be a success. He invested in stencils for the text, which wrapped around the machine's spinning ink drum. Steve hoped to make a buck or two with which to see more movies. Before he knew it, he had nine dollars in his pocket and the attention of his teachers, who forced him to give all the money back because selling anything on school property was illegal. King wasn't terribly disappointed; he was beginning to appreciate

The launching of the first American satellite, Explorer I, *from Cape Canaveral on January 31, 1958, marked the beginning of much of the country's fascination with space.*

his talents and understand what people wanted to read.

Steve took his story writing to a new level when he wrote an original story about students who took control of their school. Sensing the impact of infusing his fiction with reality, he used the names and characteristics of his friends and classmates to populate his story. And they loved it.

Steve's ever-growing interest in science fiction was inspired partly by the 1958 voyage of *Explorer I,* the first U.S. satellite to successfully orbit the Earth. Writers Ray Bradbury and Isaac Asimov were popularizing science fiction with books like *The Martian Chronicles* and *I, Robot.* Spurred on by the prevalence of this genre, Steve, at age thirteen, submitted a story to the publication *Spacemen*. It became the first of many rejected stories. He speared all his rejection slips on a large nail pounded into his bedroom wall. Chris Chesley said later, "In an odd way, they were trophies. They depressed him, but he knew that he was paying his dues." Unlike his father, Steve was persistent about his writing. When the nail could hold no more letters, he pounded a larger spike into the wall to accommodate the continuing rejections.

He and Chris spent many summer hours with several friends on the upper floor of a shed that was part of the Kings' home. There they played penny-ante card games, told stories, and smoked cigarettes until the room was blue with smoke. Sometimes he and Chris sneaked out of their bedrooms at night to sit in the cemetery near Chris's house. By the light of the moon, they read the names and dates on the gravestones.

In high school, Steve earned As and Bs in history and English classes, but Cs and Ds in science courses kept him off the honor roll. In the aftermath of "The Pit and the Pendulum" fiasco, the principal had told him he was wasting his talents writing horror and science fiction when he could have been using his intelligence and writing skills in literature or journalism. While Steve chose to ignore that advice, he did channel some of his energy into writing and editing the school newspaper. But the school paper didn't provide a release for his creative juices, so he invented his own publication—which would lead to more trouble.

It was an easy step from writing for the school news-paper to writing his own newspaper, the *Village Vomit*. In it, he poked fun at high-school athletics and home-coming, and mocked the pretentiousness of "in" and "out" cliques. King invented names for teachers, names the students would immediately recognize: Miss Raypach became Miss Rat Pack; Mr. Diehl became Old Raw Deal; the bald principal was Old Cue Ball. The administration easily found the source of this mockery. Steve had announced proudly on the masthead that he was Editor in Chief & Grand High Poobah. His punishment was to make a formal apology to each teacher and to serve two weeks in detention. At this point in his life, Steve had learned to use writing to vent his dissatisfaction with the society around him and to find acceptance among his classmates, although he still felt like an outsider. Per-haps the disapproval of adults inspired him to write and "publish" even more. Each punishment stopped him, but without lasting effect.

Luckily for Steve, the school guidance counselor recognized his talent and realized that he needed disci-pline to make the most of it. He introduced Steve to John Gould, the editor of the local newspaper, the *Lisbon Enterprise*. Gould hired Steve to cover high school sports. He earned half a cent for every word published, but far beyond any monetary value were the lessons Gould taught him about writing: "John Gould taught me more than any [English courses], and in no more than ten minutes."

For the first time in his life, Steve learned to focus his writing and to delete from his draft any material that did not directly relate to the story. He learned quickly and eagerly. He also became a baseball fan.

In 1963, Steve and Chris collaborated on a collection of stories, *People, Places, and Things—Volume 1*, described in the foreword as "an extraordinary book. It is a book for people who would enjoy being pleasantly thrilled for a few moments."

For some time, Steve had stood out as the tallest kid in school, always wearing thick glasses and dressed in any hand-me-downs his mother could find. A classmate later described him as a "big goofy kid who walked into lamp posts and telephone poles when he didn't bother to take his eyes off the book he was reading as he walked."

Steve was far from being the most popular kid in the class. He wasn't much of a jock, and his passions— writing, reading, and seeing movies—weren't the most social activities. So while he was well liked, he understood what it meant to be an outsider. He had confidence in only one aspect of his life: "I could write, and that was the way I defined myself, even as a kid."

King was especially adept at identifying other outsiders, such as the girl who had only one outfit for the entire school year. He saw how the other girls made fun of her. When she appeared at school one day in a new outfit, the teasing grew worse, a signal that those who did the teasing were unhappy she had tried to escape their ridicule. King saw her humiliation as typical of the treatment of high school students everywhere.

While Steve may not have been part of the in-crowd, he did connect with the force that was sweeping the nation: rock and roll. When he was in high school, the music of Elvis Presley, Chuck Berry, the Beatles, and many more artists captured the hearts and minds of millions of teenagers. Steve played rhythm guitar in a band called the MoonSpinners. About music, he later said, "For me, rock 'n roll was the rise of consciousness. It was like a big sun bursting over my life. That's when I really started to live."

At the time, Stephen King couldn't have known how big his own sun would burst, but he was starting to feel the changing times of the 1960s and knew he would probably change along with them.

THREE

The Art of Persistence

In 1954, Vietnam was divided along the 17th parallel into North and South Vietnam. Communist-dominated North Vietnam, with the strong support of the USSR and China, soon made inroads into weaker South Vietnam. Alarmed by the potential for communism to gain more territory, the U.S. began to send money and, soon, troops into the region.

Tensions ran high closer to home as well. In the fall of 1962, atomic weapons became a threat to America. Soviet premier Nikita Khrushchev had supplied Cuba with nuclear missiles that could easily reach the eastern coast of the United States. Although Khrushchev at first denied the presence of the missiles, President John F. Kennedy had positive proof of their existence. For several tense days, there was a standoff between the two countries. Talk of a third world war grew intense. Then Khrushchev agreed to dismantle and remove the weapons.

A year later, the unthinkable happened. The president of the United States was assassinated. On November 22, 1963, Kennedy was riding in a motorcade in Dallas, seeking support for his second run at the presidency. Three shots were fired in rapid succession. One bullet struck the president in the back of the head, and he died without regaining consciousness. Vice President Lyndon Johnson was sworn in as the thirty-sixth president. The country entered a long period of mourning, fear, and suspicion.

By 1964, the U.S. was involved in an escalating civil war in Vietnam. A year later, just before King graduated from high school, there were over 180,000 U.S. troops in the country. As American soldiers continued to pour into southeast Asia, the military draft brought fresh recruits. King and young men of his class and age all faced the very real possibility of obligatory military service after graduation.

The events of the world shook King, like everyone else, amplifying his deepest fears beyond the dark and the number thirteen. He admitted to being afraid around strangers and said he found it difficult to make friends: "There's a constant fear that I am alone." King saw the student body as divided into "winners" and "losers." He identified himself with the losers.

On the senior class trip to Washington, D.C., the

The University of Maine at Orono, where King attended college from 1966 to 1970. (University of Maine Office of Public Affairs)

knew immediately that he was in a different world—there were more students walking around the campus than there were residents in his entire hometown. Like most campuses, the college at Orono was filled with "baby boomers," children born in the post-World War II era. Soldiers had returned home to wives, fiancées, and girlfriends by the hundreds of thousands, and many started families soon thereafter.

These baby boomers shocked their parents and grandparents with their rebellion—long hair, foul language, and disrespect toward leaders and officials. Young adults demanded changes in education, values, lifestyles, laws, and entertainment. They experimented with drugs and sexual freedom. Political debates and protests against the Vietnam War were heated. Teenage males were especially intense in their protests against a system that could draft a man when he was eighteen years old but would not let him vote until he was twenty-one.

King was surprised to find that his college English teachers did not give him high marks the way his high school teachers had. His first English instructor, however, did recognize his talent and encouraged him to work harder. And that he did, spending as much free

King composing at his typewriter in the late 1960s. (David King)

time as possible writing stories and novels.

Carroll Terrell, a literature professor at the University of Maine and author of *Stephen King: Man and Artist,* remembers the day that King approached him with a thick manuscript and said that another professor had suggested he show it to Terrell. "It's a novel," said King. "I wrote it." Terrell was intrigued by this student who wrote every day and always carried a book with him. King had read more books by more different authors than any other student in his class. Terrell agreed to look over King's manuscript. He was impressed by the characters King created in *The Long Walk,* boys who embark on a walk down the length of the East Coast. The characters were natural and believable, losers in a society that gave them no help. He told King the book was remarkable and encouraged him to keep writing. But respect for his student forced Terrell to tell King the book had no chance for publication because it was a fantasy and because it did not deal with the currently popular topics of Vietnam and the peace movements. Terrell suggested that King try his hand at writing about Vietnam.

The U.S. Air Force dropped more bombs on Vietnam than had been dropped by all sides combined in World War II, and still the Americans were losing the war. The American ground troops in Vietnam—by 1968, they numbered over 500,000—were no match for the guerilla warfare of Vietnamese troops who hid in jungles, disguised themselves as peasants, and carried out devas-

Politically engaged students protested the Vietnam War on campuses stretching from the University of Maine to the University of California, Berkeley. This image was taken at the University of Wisconsin in Madison in October 1967, where students were protesting the production of napalm at a nearby chemical plant. (Courtesy of AP Photos.)

tating surprise attacks. Protests and demonstrations in the United States grew in size and frequency, and the anger increased as citizens demanded that President Lyndon Johnson bring the soldiers home. With the growing popularity of television and expanding news coverage, the networks could bring the horrors of war into the living rooms of America. Antiwar slogans were shouted everywhere; potential draftees chanted "Hell, no, we won't go" and "Give peace a chance." Millions of Americans protested in the streets. College students, including King, were the most active in protests against the war.

As he would have at most colleges, King found a divide between the students engaged politically with the times and those whose concerns were more insular and social. He wrote later, "When I was in school, Vietnam was going up in flames and Watts [a California city ravaged by race riots] and [U.S. Attorney General] Bobby Kennedy and [Reverend] Martin Luther King Jr. had been shot, and these little dollies were bopping into their eight o'clock classes with nine pounds of makeup on and their hair processed to perfection, and the high heels and everything because they wanted husbands and they wanted jobs, and they wanted all the things their mothers wanted, and they wanted to get into a big sorority. Big deal."

King started a novel about antiwar activism on a college campus. He brought the book to Terrell chapter by chapter. King finished *Sword in the Darkness* in April 1970, weeks before Ohio National Guardsmen infamously shot down several Kent State University students during a protest. With some assistance from his professors, King was able to persuade a literary agent to shop the book around for him. It was rejected by one publisher after another.

Unwilling to give up the project, he studied the manuscript to see if he could figure out what was wrong with it. He found the trouble in the cast of characters and the problems that weighed them down: tumors, out-of-wedlock pregnancy, suicide, insanity. Reading this book was not entertainment; it was a reminder of how grim life can be. Disappointed as he was, King realized that he had learned an important lesson in writing from this book. His final evaluation of the manuscript was he "couldn't even like it even when I'm drunk."

Ruth King mailed her son four dollars each week for spending money. King found out only later that sometimes she went without food to set this money aside. One thing is certain: King did not spend the money on clothes. He wore threadbare and torn clothing and did not seem to care about his appearance. Like many students of his time, King wore his hair longer than he had in high school and sometimes grew a beard.

In some ways, this was to mimic the rock stars that

By 1970, King's college experience had both politicized and radicalized the young writer. (University of Maine)

had risen to prominence during the period. King's musical tastes ran the gamut, from the popular rhythm and blues of Gladys Knight and the Pips and James Brown to the smooth singing of Elvis Presley. King also liked more rebellious acts such as Bob Dylan, Jimi Hendrix, and the Beatles. In fact, one of King's non-writing pursuits was making his own music, often acoustic and influenced by country-and-western hits. King could often be found at a local coffeehouse on open-mike night.

Next to writing, the thing King cared most about was reading. He read a book every day. As an English major, he read across a wide breadth of fiction, beginning with Thomas Hardy, Theodore Dreiser, Jack London, John Steinbeck, William Faulkner, and William Carlos Williams, who were known as naturalist writers because they wrote realistically about the human experience. This was in contrast to classic Gothic writers like Bram Stoker and Mary Shelley, who employed an ornate style in romanticizing heroes and villains in fantastical and horror stories. King still enjoyed cinema and was witness to a kind of revolution in movies as taboos on sex, violence, and language were broken down bit by bit.

In his sophomore year, King read Robert Browning's poem "Childe Roland to the Dark Tower Came," an epic about a knight named Roland whose quest is to find the Dark Tower. Part of the appeal to King was the character of protagonist, but he was equally taken with the dramatic writing:

Victorian poet Robert Browning is known for his dark, imaginative, and sometimes horrifying narrative poems. His 1855 poem "Childe Roland to the Dark Tower Came," which served as inspiration for King's epic Dark Tower series, is said to have come to him in a dream. (National Portrait Gallery, London)

> …good saints, how I feared
> To set my foot upon a dead man's cheek,
> Each step, or feel the spear I thrust to seek
> For hollows, tangled in his hair or beard!
> —It may have been a water-rat I speared,
> But, ugh! It sounded like a baby's shriek.

That poem would become the core of King's Dark Tower series, which he would work on for over thirty years.

During the summer of 1969, King took a job at the university library. One day, he had lunch on the lawn with fellow workers and met Tabitha Spruce, another library employee. King liked her laugh and especially her tendency to swear "like a millworker instead of a coed." As luck would have it, she was a writer too.

King took a poetry workshop (where students share their own work to help each other improve) the following fall, his senior year. Tabitha, or "Tabby," was in the room on the first day. Impressed by her poetry, King soon developed a crush on the petite brunette. They started dating, finding in each other common interests and enthusiasms.

King sometimes hung out at a place called the Coffee House. While there on Halloween, somebody asked King to read one of his stories. As he read, he was pleased that the audience seemed so engrossed. Then some people in the audience laughed at a point where he didn't see anything funny in the story. It took him weeks to figure out they were laughing to relieve tension, which sometimes becomes necessary when people enter a surreal world. "Everything funny is horrible, and everything horrible is funny," he realized. He also realized that sometimes when someone is hurt we laugh because we are so glad we are not the one who is hurt. The fact that he was able to touch people so thoroughly with his writing was a great source of encouragement.

King's narratives often employed dark, disturbing story lines that included seduction and rape, blackmail, suicide, riots, dysfunctional families, and human weaknesses. Many professors who read his work during college had the same advice for him: he should put his considerable writing talent to work on something more "serious" since, they said, he would tire of writing horror when he was mature. King was not surprised by these comments. His metaphor for the horror writer was: "If you visualize American literature as a town, then the horror writer's across the tracks on the poor side of town, and that's where 'nice' people won't go."

In 1969, King wrote a column titled "King's Garbage Truck" for the college newspaper, the *Maine Campus*. Essentially, he could write about whatever he wanted and took the opportunity to touch on a wide variety of subjects and political attitudes. He supported strikers in California vineyards, protested the United States' involvement in the Vietnam War, and reviewed movies, television shows, and music. He did not hesitate to criticize campus clubs and fraternities or to satirize groups considered "in" and "out." He annoyed other staffers by showing up at the last minute before deadline. One fellow writer said, "Steve would come in and sit down at the typewriter and produce two flawless pages of copy. He carries stories around in his head the way most people carry change in their pockets."

King took courses in English and American literature, creative writing, play production, and writing for radio and TV. He also took courses in education and psychology to assure himself of a job in teaching after graduation if his writing could not sustain him. When the English department asked students for suggestions for new courses, King criticized the school for lacking a course on popular culture. Because he spoke so eloquently and passionately about the topic, he was asked to teach "Popular Literature and Culture" with another professor. Twenty-one-year-old King was the first undergraduate in the history of the school to teach a course.

Part of the education curriculum included a stint of student teaching. King worked at a private school, Hampden Academy, in a town near Bangor. Hampden was much more conservative than the University of Maine. As soon as he arrived on the campus, he was ordered by an administrator to cut his hair. He did not. He wrote a column about that incident for the *Maine Campus:* "Can you imagine a country supposedly based on freedom of expression telling people that they can't grow hair on their head or face?" He listed criminals who had short hair and asked if everybody should look like them.

Like other young men graduating from college, King was required to register for the military draft. The military excused him from service with a 4F rating because of high blood pressure, limited vision, flat feet, and punctured eardrums. He was free to keep writing.

Around the time King finished *Sword in the Darkness,* and inspired by Browning's poem, he began work on *The Dark Tower.* Typing as always with two fingers, he tapped out the first line of a work of fiction that would evolve over thirty years: "The man in black fled across the desert, and the gunslinger followed." The novel, subtitled *The Gunslinger,* features Roland searching for the man in black across a post-apocalyptic landscape. The man in black is responsible for destroying Roland's life by wiping out everything and everyone he cared for. Roland seeks revenge and, in the process, the Dark Tower. King wrote five stories, all of which were published in the *Magazine of Fantasy and Science Fiction* and became chapters in the multi-volume novel.

King graduated in the spring of 1970 with a bachelor's degree in English, a minor in speech, and a certificate to teach secondary education. When he first went to college he had been a conservative Methodist from a small town, a registered Republican who unquestioningly supported his government's policies in Vietnam. The political climate at the University of Maine awakened King politically. He had become an antiwar protester. He was also made aware that he had grown up in a somewhat dysfunctional family, living in poverty with a single parent. The strong liberal social values he espoused in college would become a hallmark of his writing.

Before he entered higher education, his mother had warned him that a writing career might be difficult at best. His experiences at the university—the serious criticism of his work, the rejection of his novel at many publishing houses—drove home that fact. But King refused to be daunted. Little did he know that the biggest challenges to his dream of being a writer were still ahead.

FOUR

The Success of Horror

A fter graduation, King could not find a teaching job, so he took the only available work he could find: pumping gas for $1.25 an hour and providing a free loaf of bread to each customer getting a full tank. He quit pumping gas when he found a job in a laundry for $1.60 an hour. This job presented challenges to even the strongest of stomachs. Linens from restaurants, caked in decomposing food, were crawling with maggots. Hospital bedsheets were often covered with blood or other mysterious stains. The best King could do was hold his nose and keep working.

Less than a year after graduation, on January 2, 1971, King and Tabby Spruce married. They chose Saturday for the ceremony because the laundry was not open Saturday afternoon. Steve skipped work that Saturday morning to have the entire day free to celebrate. They moved into a rented trailer near the university, hoping to move out when Tabby finished her bachelor's degree in history and could get a good job. But the good job did not materialize, and she took a job as a waitress at a doughnut shop.

Times were tight for the newlyweds. King had little time or energy to work on his writing. Although the ideas kept streaming into his head, the burden of unpaid bills and the exhaustion from stress and discouragement made it difficult for King to even bring himself to work on *The Dark Tower* manuscript that he had begun with enthusiasm just months before. The fact that the drinking he'd started on his senior class trip had developed into a habit added to his woes.

King did complete some stories, usually at night and sometimes during his lunch hour. He sent them primarily to men's magazines such as *Adam, Gent, Penthouse,* and *Cavalier.* While some of these magazines required racy content to compliment their explicit pictorials, others required only a good story. And the upside of these magazines was the pay—$200 to $300 upon publication, a lot of money when King was making about sixty dollars a week at the laundry.

King wanted to show his published stories to his mother, but he didn't want her to see the sexually oriented pictures and ads in the magazines. He photocopied the stories and cut out the ads around them before he sent them to her.

A son, Joseph, was born a year after Naomi. The Kings struggled to buy diapers and food, pay medical bills, keep up with the telephone bill, and repair their old car. King wrote as often as he could, sitting in the tiny furnace room of their double-wide trailer, typing on Tabby's Olivetti typewriter. He completed a manuscript he called *Getting It On,* a hostage story he had begun in high school, but was unable to sell it. Although he enjoyed teaching, King was still trying to believe he could someday be a full-time writer: "There I was, unpublished, living in a trailer, with barely enough money to get by and increasing doubt in my abilities as a writer."

Soon, his predicament seemed insolvable. Their phone was shut off. Their seven-year-old car needed very expensive repairs. The only way King could make money as a writer was by selling novels, not short stories. He could not write novels without long stretches of free time, so he tried to write faster. He wrote a book-length manuscript, *The Running Man,* over a long weekend. In writing it, King was like the story's hero, in a race against time, gambling to see if his efforts would pay off, and pay well. But King was not able to sell the book, so he shoved it away in a trunk getting heavier with old manuscripts, including *Getting It On.* Still, he would not give up his dream.

Without significant time to invest in a novel, King started small and worked at growing an idea. He began with a character, a high school girl named Carrie. As he started the book, he was enthusiastic about the idea that high school is a place of almost bottomless bigotry. Carrie is an outcast who figures out a way to get revenge on those who torment her. King recalled some of his fellow students from his high school experiences, specifically the girl who had only one outfit for the entire year and received an onslaught of abuse for it.

A former coworker, obsessive in her religion and often quoting biblical passages, triggered King to wonder: what if she had a child and forbade her to do anything fun, but the child refused to accept her religious obsession? This person, in part, became Carrie's mother.

King's enthusiasm for the idea lasted through a few pages. Then, disgusted, he threw the draft into the trash. Tabby, one of his best critics, rescued it, read it, and encouraged him to finish it. He realized that the reason he felt frustrated about the story was that he had not delved deeply enough into Carrie's life, so his heroine did not seem real even to him. He searched his memory for unpopular girls in his high school classes. He found them waiting for him with details such as a missing button replaced with a paper clip and sweat stains on a white blouse. He also found memories of scenes of teasing and humiliation by fellow students. His former college instructor, Carroll Terrell, explains the King magic that happened next. King asked himself the question: what would I think and feel if this happened to me? Then he produced the emotions in himself and became

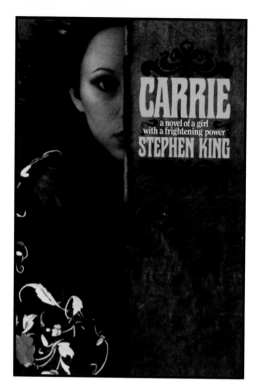

King's debut novel, Carrie, *published in 1974.*

on the line with amazing news. The paperback rights to *Carrie,* which King had hoped would sell but couldn't be certain, had sold for $400,000 to New American Library publishers. King would split that sum with Doubleday. In the blink of an eye, after knowing no other life but one of poverty, King was rich.

He desperately wanted to share the news with Tabby, but she was en route to the house. King walked into town—he hadn't bought her anything for Mother's Day yet. Not much was available, so he bought her a hair dryer for $16.95. She held it in her arms as she cried at the news of their newfound fortune.

Carrie saw publication in 1974 but did not sell well at first. Chief among the criticisms was its bloody repulsiveness. However, all but one reviewer highly recommended the book as exciting. The dissenter, *Library*

Journal, called it "a contender for the bloodiest book of the year—menstrual blood, blood of childbirth and miscarriage, blood of a whole town dying, and finally the lifeblood of the heroine draining away." Much of the mail King received about the book was from high school boys and girls who said they identified with the main character. Gradually the book became popular, selling 3.5 million copies.

With the advance from the paperback contract, King felt free to leave his teaching job, but he wasn't sure he wanted to. He had enjoyed his two years of working with his students, especially the five whom he was mentoring as they wrote novels. Finally he made the decision to quit teaching and write: "Good, bad, or indifferent books, that's for others to decide . . . it's enough to *write.*"

King now had money left over for things he couldn't previously afford, including alcohol. His drinking increased, both in amount and frequency. The death of his mother at the end of 1973 tempered the high of success and wealth. He gave the eulogy at her funeral and later said, "I think I did a pretty good job, considering how drunk I was." He told himself he was not an alcoholic, that he just liked to drink. Because he was a sensitive person, he said, he needed alcohol to face the horrors of everyday life.

King kept writing, about 1,500 words a day. The idea for his next book, originally called *Second Coming* before being retitled *'Salem's Lot,* came directly from a course he taught at the University of Maine called

The grand and remote Stanley Hotel in Estes Park, Colorado, served as the inspiration for King's terrifying 1977 novel, The Shining.

his own experience to describe a man who felt inadequate as a parent. He had become a father without the advantage of having grown up with a father: "The first time I realized that parents are not always good was when the kid wouldn't stop crying in the middle of the night. I was getting up to get the kid a bottle, and somewhere in the back of my mind, in some sewer back there, an alligator stirs . . . *make it stop crying. You know how to do it—use the pillow."*

It took King many years to realize he was also depicting his own personal dysfunction as a drinker and failing parent and husband. The fact that Jack Torrance was a failed writer as compared to King's growing success served only as a mild misdirection.

After reading the manuscript, his editor warned, "First

the telekinetic girl, *then* vampires, *now* the haunted hotel and the telepathic kid. You're gonna get typed." King answered, "That's OK, Bill, I'll be a horror writer if that's what people want. That's just fine." Though King knew the literary establishment would sneer at horror fiction, he wasn't troubled by being labeled a genre writer. In 1977, *The Shining* outpaced the sales of both his first two novels.

In 1976, a film version of *Carrie* was released and became a box-office success. Both Sissy Spacek, playing Carrie, and Piper Laurie, playing Carrie's mother, were nominated for Academy Awards. The movie grossed $30 million just in the United States. King criticized the movie version because the producers did not let the movie character Carrie destroy the whole town, as the book character had done. Still, this movie brought increased attention and sales to King. It was the first of almost fifty King books and stories that have appeared as major motion pictures or television miniseries.

At this time, King was finishing two or three manuscripts a year. His publisher did not want to put that many of his books out at once, fearing that the market for King's work would soon be saturated and potential readers would ignore them. King, however, could not stop writing. His answer was to publish under the pseudonym Richard Bachman. He enjoyed the anonymity, and he eventually published five novels under that name. He worked again on the hostage story *Getting It On*. It became *Rage*, the first Bachman book, and one that sold

FIVE

Terrorizing the Reader . . . and Writer

With the 1978 publication of a fourth blockbuster novel, *The Stand,* King had become a bona fide star. *The Stand* was quite possibly the most popular of King's novels. It was a huge book, 400,000 words long even after King cut nearly 100,000 words from the original manuscript. King resented what he considered heavy editing, but he did not have the leverage to fight the changes. All the same, this author, who as a boy had walked to a nearby well to fetch water because his house didn't have indoor plumbing, was now a millionaire.

Somebody asked him what he did with all his money. "I don't really do anything with it," he said, "except to buy books and awful socks like the ones I'm wearing and stuff like that. . . . I have a business manager in New York and he invests in things." It did, however, provide King with opportunity. One such option was another change of scenery, this time across the Atlantic Ocean. He wanted to write a good old-fashioned English ghost story.

After King finished *The Stand* but prior to its publication, the Kings advertised in a London newspaper: "Wanted: a draughty Victorian house in the country with dark attic and creaking floorboards, preferably haunted." They moved to Fleet, Hampshire, not too far from London. Naomi and Joseph enrolled in local schools, and Tabby took care of the new baby, seven-month-old Owen. While in Fleet, Steve and Tabby met Peter Straub. Straub, a few years older than King, also wrote supernatural stories. The men knew of each other's work.

This map of southern England and Wales shows the town of Fleet in Hampshire, located about forty miles southwest of London.

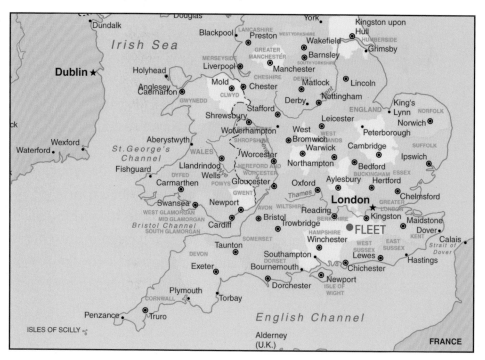

Straub was an expatriate writer, living in London for seven years before returning to New York City, whose best-known book is *Ghost Story*. The two men discussed their hopes that horror and supernatural fiction would become more acceptable in the broad field of literature.

During his three months in England, King did not conjure what he had hoped. The family returned to America, where King eagerly accepted an offer from the University of Maine in Orono to teach one course in creative writing. An appealing aspect of the job was that, for the first time in his life, King would have an office. Although he found that he spent little time in his office because of the demands of the classroom, he enjoyed teaching his course, Themes in Supernatural Literature.

Although he was no longer King's editor, Bill Thompson presented him with a project in November 1978. Thompson suggested that King write a book about why people are attracted to horror in books, movies, radio, and TV. King's first impulse was to refuse, since he had never written book-length nonfiction and because "the thought of having to tell the truth was intimidating." On the other hand, maybe he could answer once and for all the question he was continually asked: why do you write material that makes your readers uncomfortable? His often-repeated answer was that he wrote horror stories because he loved to scare people and people love to be scared. Besides, his research for the book would help him teach his class in supernatural literature. That project became *Danse Macabre*. In his foreword to the book, King tells his readers, "Maybe there will be something here to make you think or make you laugh or just make you mad. Any of those reactions would please me. Boredom, however, would be a bummer." He stated his goal for the book succinctly: "I recognize terror as the finest emotion, and so I will try to terrorize the reader. But if I find that I cannot terrify, I will try to horrify, and if I find that I cannot horrify, I'll go for the gross-out. I'm not proud."

The book is sometimes called a "horror textbook," a guided tour of the primary horror art forms, including books, movies, TV shows, radio programs, and comic books between 1950 and the late 1970s. He explains his title: "The good horror tale will dance its way to the center of your life and find the secret door to the room you believed no one but you knew of."

The *Birmingham News* review summed up the book: "*Danse Macabre* is a conversation with Steve King . . . it's easygoing. . . . At the same time it's perceptive and knowledgeable, a visit with a craftsman who has honed his skills to an edge that cuts clean and sparkles with brilliance."

King's reasons for writing horror in the foreword to *Danse Macabre* are entertaining but perhaps slightly tongue in cheek. In 2003, upon receiving the Distinguished Contribution to American Letters Award from the National Book Foundation, King discussed more seriously his reasons for writing:

Now, there are lots of people who will tell you that anyone who writes genre fiction or any kind of fiction that tells a story is in it for the money and nothing else. It's a lie. The idea that all storytellers are in it for the money is untrue but it is still hurtful, it's infuriating and it's demeaning. I never in my life wrote a single word for money. As badly as we needed money, I never wrote for money. From those early days to this gala black tie night, I never once sat down at my desk thinking today I'm going to make a hundred grand. Or this story will make a great movie. . . . My wife knows the importance of this award isn't the recognition of being a great writer or even a good writer but the recognition of being an honest writer.

Frank Norris, the author of *McTeague*, said something like this: "What should I care if they, i.e., the critics, single me out for sneers and laughter? I never truckled, I never lied. I told the truth." And that's always been the bottom line for me. The story and the people in it may be make believe but I need to ask myself over and over if I've told the truth about the way real people would behave in a similar situation. . . .

. . . We understand that fiction is a lie to begin with. To ignore the truth inside the lie is to sin against the craft, in general, and one's own work in particular.

I'm sure I've made the wrong choices from time to time. . . . I have revised the lie out if I could and that's far more important. When readers are deeply entranced by a story, they forget the storyteller completely. The tale is all they care about. . . .

How stringently the writer holds to the truth inside the lie is one of the ways that he can judge how seriously he takes his craft. My wife, who doesn't seem to know how to [tell] a lie even in a social context where people routinely say things like, "You look wonderful, have you lost weight?" has always understood these things without needing to have them spelled out. She's what the Bible calls a pearl beyond price. She also understands why I was in those early days so often bitterly angry at writers who were considered "literary." I knew I didn't have quite enough talent or polish to be one of them so there was an element of jealousy, but I was also infuriated by how these writers always seemed to have the inside track in my view at that time.

Danse Macabre offered King a chance to communicate directly with his readers as well as a chance to make a case for the legitimacy of the writing he did. King knew writers of horror fiction were often considered second-class citizens by the literary world, but he didn't buy that theory. He remained committed to doing the kind of writing that he liked, regardless of what the critics said.

His next idea for a story appeared when Naomi's cat, Smucky, was killed by a speeding car. Smucky was not the first local animal to meet its demise this way. The neighborhood children had dedicated a part of the yard to animal burial and posted a sign reading "pet sematary." They gave each animal a brief and solemn service before burying it. King wondered: what if the dead came back to life? This idea became the focus for his book *Pet Sematary.*

In the novel, protagonist Louis Creed knows the otherwise secret information that anything that is buried in a nearby Micmac Indian tribal burial ground comes back to life. However, resurrection is only of the body; the corpse changes personality entirely. This is what happens to Creed's son Gage. After he dies and comes back to life, he is a demon who kills both his brother and his mother. The already horrifying story escalates when Creed's wife comes back from the dead.

In *Pet Sematary,* King tackled head-on the issue of death: "Death is it. The one thing we all have to face. Two hundred years from now there won't be any of us up walking around and taking nourishment. . . . For a long time, death has been one of the great unmentionables in our society, along with sex and how much money you make. It's generally something you try to keep from the kids."

The novel allowed King to open up to a fear he shares with every parent alive: the death of a son or daughter. And King tackled it in a "worst-case analysis" approach. The horror of the death of a child in the manuscript so terrified King that he did not submit the book for publication until three years after he wrote it.

Publishers Weekly said of the book, "The last 50 pages are so terrifying, one might try to make it through them without a breath—but what is most astonishing here is how much besides horror is here."

With each new title, Stephen King was literally reinventing the horror genre. He was the acknowledged master of horror fiction and set the bar high for aspiring writers. Still, he was conscious of the debt he owed those who came before, including William Golding, whose 1954 masterpiece *Lord of the Flies* still sends shivers down the spines of school children everywhere.

Castle Rock was the name of a town in that novel and the town remained in King's memory from the time he first read the book. His depiction of a town he named Castle Rock became the setting for his novel *The Dead Zone,* which was published in 1979. King had wondered: What if a man had the ability to see into the future? Johnny Smith, King's main character in *The Dead Zone*, awakens from a five-year coma with the psychic power of precognition. When he becomes aware of a plan to unleash nuclear war, he must choose between sacrificing himself and sacrificing many people. Readers said the end was particularly moving and called this a tragic story, not a horror story. *The Dead Zone* was the first of King's books to be number one on the *New York Times* bestseller list.

Events of the late 1970s, specifically the Soviet invasion of Afghanistan, raised questions about America's international responsibilities. President Jimmy Carter condemned the Soviet move and the Cold War heated up again. Ronald Reagan, who defeated Carter in the 1980 election, called the Soviet Union an evil empire and placed cruise missiles in North Atlantic Treaty Organization (NATO) countries. Ultimately, the most powerful nuclear weapons in the world pointed towards each

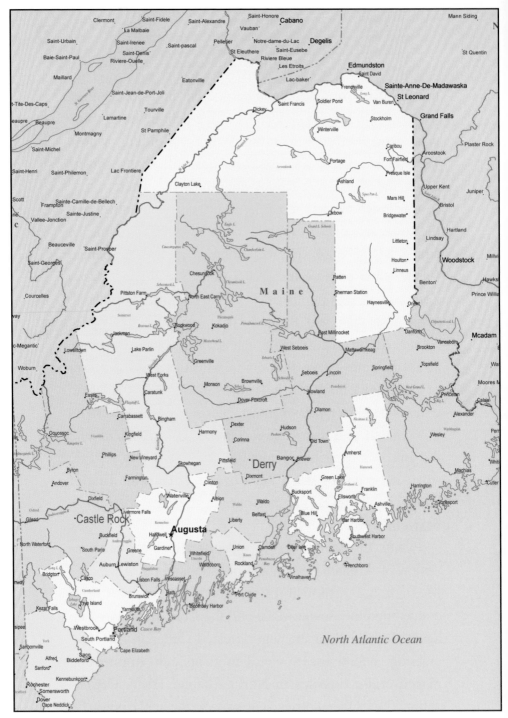

The state of Maine, with actual towns marked in black and the location of two of King's famous fictional towns in red.

other. Protests against nuclear weapons erupted around the world. Conflict between Americans who agreed with Reagan's policy and those who did not spurred protests, demonstrations, fear, and paranoia. The two countries finally agreed to resolve the situation after a number of tense years, leading to a 1987 treaty that limited the spread of weapons. King elaborated on that paranoia in his 1980 novel *Firestarter,* which imagined an evil government agency that conducted secret experiments with narcotics on unsuspecting children—with horrifying results.

King's influence on America was widespread. His books had become instant bestsellers. Hardcovers, like *Firestarter,* shattered six-figure sales (285,000 copies). Once a King book went to paperback, it would sell in the millions.

Adding to the revenue stream were movie rights. By 1980, three of his books had been turned into films (*'Salem's Lot* was a made-for-TV movie). The American public couldn't get enough of King's work.

With such selling power comes much authority. King's editors seldom questioned him about his books. However, *Cujo,* published in 1981 and the second novel set in fictional Castle Rock, features a rabid 200-pound St. Bernard that kills a four-year-old boy. King's editors asked him to change the ending so the child would not die. "That's not negotiable," King answered immediately, "the kid died." However, a few years later when *Cujo* was being made into a movie, the director asked King if Tad had to die. King said no, the director could change that part, because he now wanted to see what would happen if Tad lived.

The month after *Cujo* came out, King published a collection of four novellas titled *Different Seasons*. Two of the most popular were "Rita Hayworth and the Shawshank Redemption" and "Apt Pupil." The "Shawshank Redemption" characters include sadistic prison guards, violent rapists, corrupt bureaucrats, and adulterous wives. Andy Dufresne, the main character of the story, is sentenced to life in prison for a murder he did not commit. In prison, he is tortured by brutal fellow

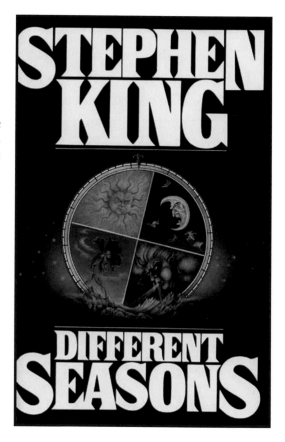

The cover of the 1982 novella collection Different Seasons, *which includes some of Stephen King's most acclaimed works.*

inmates and turned down for parole time after time. The Rita Hayworth connection focuses on what seems like a simple request by Dufresne for a poster of the movie star Rita Hayworth. An escape plan, a hidden box of money, and agonizingly elaborate descriptions of the brutality of the prison setting make this one of King's most unforgettable tales. Critics noted that in this story, unlike in most of King's other work, the main character is brutalized by other people, not by supernatural forces.

The movie version of the novella, shortened to *The Shawshank Redemption,* would come out many years later and would be one of the most successful translations of a King story to film. The movie's narrative stayed very close to the original story's. Despite receiving a warm reception from prominent critics across the country, its box-office take was less than overwhelming. It did, however, enjoy tremendous life as a video rental and in showings on cable television.

In "Apt Pupil," King asks: how could the Nazis systematically and in cold blood torture and kill as they did in the Holocaust? The tale is made even more gruesome as thirteen-year-old Todd, the story's protagonist, becomes fascinated as he learns firsthand that his neighbor, Arthur Denker, was a commander in a Nazi death camp during the Holocaust. At first their friendship is just a simple one between an old man and a young man. As Denker reveals his secret, the reader watches Todd experience feelings alternating between suspicion and fascination. The two develop a need for each other: Todd needs Denker to feed his need for macabre scenes, and Denker needs Todd to keep his secret.

When asked about the story, King answered, "I certainly didn't find evil seductive in any sick way—that would be pathological—but I did find it compelling. And I think most people do, or the bookstores wouldn't still be filled with biographies of [Adolf] Hitler more than 35 years after World War Two." Still people asked King why he wrote about horror. He said, "Sooner or later, my mind always seems to turn back in that direction, God knows why." As readers and critics sought to find answers, King shrugged off their search and continued to listen to questions.

King is an avid and tireless explorer. Though he was happy to be a horror writer, *Different Seasons* showcased a different King. It was an experiment born out of confidence in his storytelling abilities that relied less on the wild and fantastic, and found resolution more grounded in everyday reality.

In 1982, King also experimented with collaboration. In scenes reminiscent of his collaboration with Chris Chesley in elementary school, he and his friend Peter Straub, whose company he had enjoyed in England, began work on a book. Apparently they inspired each other. They sent text from one computer to another as fast as they could type it out. When one of them wanted to stop writing, he simply sent the manuscript to the other writer, who picked up the story where it left off. The collaboration worked so seamlessly that King said about the book, "When I worked on my half of the copy editing, I went through large chunks of the manuscript unsure myself who had written what." The result was *The Talisman*, the story of a search for a magical medical cure. The characters in this adventure are often compared to the characters in J. R. R. Tolkien's *The Lord of the Rings*.

As King's popularity grew, so did criticisms of his work. Many reviewers scoffed, declaring that horror books were inherently less worthy than books of other genres. Some critics said that his books were nothing more than good stories with no depth of thought and without the level of language that distinguishes literature that lasts through the ages. Others complained that his novels were too long and could be greatly improved with cutting. On the positive side, critics noted that his characters face the same kinds of problems most of us face. They appreciated his special focus on people who are shunned by others. King is often self-deprecating in his assessment of his work, but he won't back down from his confidence in his storytelling ability.

With Ronald Reagan, an economics-minded president, in the White House, the wealth of the country surged, and Americans embraced an aggressive habit of consumption. King's life took a parallel route. While he could do many great things with words and imagination, what King couldn't do was limit his consumption of beer. Some nights he was able to stop drinking while he was sober enough to go to bed and sleep. Other nights he would get up after he had gone to bed and finish off all the beer he could find. He developed a drug habit along with his alcohol addiction and learned to hide this additional vice in public, functioning at a fairly competent level. In retrospect, he believes that he was an alcoholic when he wrote *The Shining* and addicted to drugs as well as alcohol when he wrote *The Tommyknockers* in 1986. He said later that he hardly remembers writing *Cujo*.

He was brought face-to-face with his problem when the state of Maine enacted a returnable can/bottle law. Instead of throwing empty beer containers into the trash, Tabby saved them for return. The box of returns clearly showed that Steve was drinking as much as a case of sixteen-ounce beers in a single night. When confronted, he admitted that he had a problem.

Tabby dumped all his cocaine, baggies, valium, and other pills in front of him to show the extent of his drug use. She called together a group of family and friends who stood by her as she told Steve he would either go to a rehabilitation center or he would have to leave the house. She said she and his kids loved him, but that they would not stand by while he killed himself.

King was faced with a difficult choice. He had achieved much of his success as a writer while addicted. He was not sure he could write well while completely sober. Yet he knew that Tabby would not allow him to live with his family if he were drinking or using drugs. He believed he was going to have to choose between his writing and his family.

The history of the twentieth century's literary canon is filled with stories of brilliance dampened by gross excess. Ernest Hemingway, F. Scott Fitzgerald, Dylan Thomas, and William Faulkner all battled addictions to alcohol. Fitzgerald ultimately drank himself to death, as did Thomas. King had to convince himself, like those great writers hadn't been able to, that his talents and skills were not poured from a bottle. It would take him time, but he did.

SIX

Bestsellasaurus Rex

B y the mid-1980s, the King franchise was rolling
full steam ahead. King had been writing for well
over twenty years, and enjoying huge success for the
previous dozen or so. It made sense that he would be
interested in a diversion from sitting down at the key-
board every day. He certainly had earned enough money
to take a chance and enough respect to receive one.

That opportunity came in the spring of 1985 from the
famous movie producer Dino DeLaurentis, who had
already been involved in a number of film adaptations
of King's work. He talked the writer into directing the
film adaptation of "Trucks," which had appeared in the
1978 short-story collection *Night Shift* after making its
debut in a 1973 issue of *Cavalier*. It is the story of people
trapped in a diner when trucks take on minds of their own

with plans to enslave the human race. King wrote the screenplay before directing the movie, which was re-titled *Maximum Overdrive*. He started the project optimistically: "I thought it was time I took a crack at doing Steve King. . . . After all, if you want it done right, you have to do it yourself."

Like many of his fans, he had been disappointed with the great director Stanley Kubrick's production of *The Shining*. After seeing that film, he summarized his feelings toward it: "It's like this great big gorgeous car with no engine in it—that's all." He said Kubrick had ignored the subtext of the book, which was the disintegration of a family. He also disapproved of the choice of Jack Nicholson as the star, believing him to have been typecast from other movies.

King had the opportunity to attempt what he had wished Kubrick had done—rendering the themes of the work as King had written it. In preparation for directing the movie, King had in his office a model of the diner where much of the action takes place. He created miniature scenes there with toy trucks and figurines made of lead. This helped but did not prepare him sufficiently for the myriad problems of directing, like an actor who was too scared to play a scene in which a driverless truck would back him up to a gas pump, trapping him. To show that it was safe, King allowed himself to be pushed by the truck. Convinced, the actor then did the scene.

The shoot took place in North Carolina during the summer of 1985. The brutal heat of the South should have been enough to exhaust King, but he took on more work on top of the movie. After shooting all day, he would stop at a local fast food restaurant for supper and spend the rest of the evening in his rented home working on revisions of his forthcoming novel *It*. He spent four frustrating months with such a schedule. King said, "I would leave in the morning and I would see the sun just coming up in the left rear view of my motorcycle, bright red. And when I left the set . . . I would see it going *down* red in the right-hand mirror of my motorcycle."

While he was working on the movie, interviewers asked him about the money he made. He said he didn't think much about it. He spent $2.77 a day at McDonald's for breakfast. The rest of the time he brought takeout

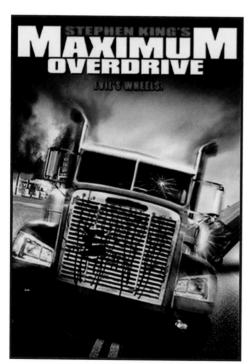

A promotional movie poster for the 1986 King-directed film starring Emilio Estevez and Yeardley Smith, who went on to later fame as the voice of Lisa Simpson on The Simpsons.

home or ate on the set. One day he realized that he was walking around with several thousand dollars in his pants pockets. When asked how he felt about being as rich as he was, he said he thought all money was good for was to give a person a little more security. He was paid $70,000 to direct the movie—a large sum of money to many people. But King could have made much more staying home and writing another book. He chose the movie because it piqued his curiosity.

Despite the problems with directing, King found humor in some of the work. He appreciated challenges, like figuring out how to show blood spurting from a dummy. (The answer was to tuck a freezer bag filled with ketchup under the dummy's shirt. When a steamroller ran over the dummy, "blood" spurted all over.) Every once in a while, a trucker would turn into the movie set, not realizing that the other trucks, the gas pumps, and the diner were fake. King remembers one such incident: "This guy comes in . . . we had blown up this toilet paper truck. It was ripped in half, there was burned toilet paper all over everything, there's garbage spread all over its body, there's a blown-up beer truck, there's a blown-up garbage truck . . . He goes 'You really serve beer here? Can I get a hamburger?'"

The one downside was the fact that shooting took King away from his family. He won't do it again, he said, "not under any circumstances while I have children that I can enjoy and a wife that I can enjoy. It would be one thing if she were a bitch . . . and if the kids were a bunch of spoiled rotten little monsters . . . the fact is that I like them better than the job."

Despite the long hours and hard work, *Maximum Overdrive* did not meet any critical acclaim, nor did it do well commercially. King was used to criticism, however, and he knew that huge sales did not necessarily translate into roaring appreciation. *The Talisman*, which he coauthored with Peter Straub, hit the markets in 1984 with a $500,000 advertising budget. Although the book was on the bestseller list for seven months, many fans and critics alike declared that the combination of styles did not work and that they preferred to read books by just one of the writers. Contrary to what King thought, some critics said the story shuffled awkwardly back and forth between King's bold and brassy style and Straub's less emotional writing. These critics agreed with the reviewer in *People* magazine, who wrote, "In horror fiction, two heads are better than one only if they're on the same body."

But no bad review or box-office flop could reverse King's surge in popularity. He was the best-known writer in the country. Up until 1982, he had complained both publicly and privately that he could not go anywhere without being recognized and mobbed. He had his tongue in his cheek when he acted in a television commercial for the American Express credit card. In the commercial, he slinks around in a haunted mansion, dressed in an after-dinner jacket, and complains, "When I'm not recognized, it just kills me. So instead of saying, 'I wrote

Carrie,' I carry the American Express card—without it, isn't life a little scary? The American Express card—don't leave home without it."

The commercial would make the writer even more famous, despite his frustration with publicity. People stopped and stared at him in restaurants and on the street. He spoke of being in a mall and hearing people whisper, "That's Stephen King." He said, "That's just what paranoid people start to hear just before the men in the white coats take them away."

The gawking didn't stop once the family was behind closed doors. The Kings had purchased a beautiful old Italianate home in Bangor, Maine, in the early 1980s.

The Kings' home in Bangor, Maine. (Courtesy of AP Photos.)

King believed he could use the location as a model for the fictional town known as Derry in his stories. But the house really became something of a horror. The citizens of Bangor accepted King as he wished to be and mostly left him alone. But fans—the term derives from the word fanatic, meaning marked by excessive enthusiasm—descended on the Bangor home with abandon. The Kings had to erect huge metal gates around the property to keep people at bay. And the family had to leave town every year on Halloween. "I hate Halloween," he says. "I've turned into America's giant pumpkin and I can't relate to that."

Even the last shred of anonymity King possessed was taken away from him. The Richard Bachman secret was uncovered by a bookstore clerk who did a copyright search at the Library of Congress. The slipup at the publishing house had lingered all these years, and King's name appeared on the registration form of *Rage*. When the clerk approached him, King knew he could not deny the truth any more. Already, close readers of King's work had noticed and wrote about serious similarities between Bachman's and King's writing. King became angry at the additional attention: "I was pissed. It's like you can't have anything. . . . Why should anyone care? It's like they wait to find stuff out, particularly if it's something you don't want people to know." He attributed the "death" of Bachman to "cancer of the pseudonym."

Still, King's outing prompted the 1985 publication of *The Bachman Books,* with credit this time given to

Stephen King. With immediate, positive fan reaction, the book's success proved that the American public could not get enough of King's work. Between 1985 and 1987, seven King books were published, and six movies made from King's stories or novels appeared either on the big screen or on television.

In 1970, King had sold five chapters of a science fiction/western for serial publication in *The Magazine of Fantasy and Science Fiction*. In the early 1980s his editor wanted him to publish those chapters and others in a multi-volume series. King disagreed. He said that no one would read a book about a gunslinger named Roland of Gilead. The editor worked on the project despite King's objections. He hired an excellent illustrator who produced full-color endpapers, color illustrations, and black-and-white page decorations. His cover painting portrays the gunslinger at sunset with a large crow on his shoulder and the Dark Tower showing through the mist behind him. King worried that readers might be disappointed that he was going off in a new direction with this series. They might prefer that he stick with books about contemporary characters in contemporary settings. They might feel that he was simply writing an old cowboy western. He need not have worried. The books became as popular as his earlier horror stories. When he saw how fast they sold, he admitted that he was a "Bestsellasaurus Rex . . . I started out as a storyteller. Along the way I have become an economic force as well."

Putnam Publishing issued a collection of King's short stories titled *Skeleton Crew*. At the end of the book, King added a section in which he told the origin of each story. These notes added charm and interest, especially for devoted fans of King who were curious about his writing process. An example is the way he described the genesis of "The Mist": "I was halfway down the middle aisle looking for hot dog buns, when I imagined a big prehistoric bird flapping its way toward the meat counter at the back, knocking over cans of pineapple chunks and tomato sauce. By the time my son Joe and I were in the checkout lane, I was amusing myself with a story about all these people trapped in a supermarket surrounded by prehistoric animals." Contrary to many predictions, this story collection sold 600,000 copies, as many as could be expected from a best-selling novel. This proved that a collection could do as well in the market as a novel— if the author was Stephen King.

Such was King's name recognition that when a movie, *Stand by Me,* was made from King's novella "The Body"— a more traditional story missing much of his trademark horror and fantasy—the movie's producers and publicists made an effort to downplay King's name so moviegoers wouldn't assume it was another blood and guts story. King was deeply moved when he first saw the film. At the end of the showing, King excused himself. After about fifteen minutes, he returned and said that the story had been the story of his life. It was highly emotional for him to see his childhood friends

A movie poster for the hit 1986 film Stand by Me.

come back to life. This movie, apart from all those that had been made from his books, captured his original voice. Audiences loved *Stand by Me*.

An obvious indicator of King's place in popular culture as well as the history of literature was the appearance of Douglas Winter's biography and study *Stephen King: The Art of Darkness*. This was the first of many books about King, a collection that includes biographies, trivia, collections of interviews, encyclopedias, and bibliographies.

By now, King needed a secretary to handle his ever-increasing influx of mail. He asked a staff member to create a publication to answer the five hundred or so mail inquiries he received each week. King's new staff published an informal newsletter titled *Castle Rock* "to keep you up-to-date on the work of this prolific writer."

No matter how often King talked about why he wrote horror and why people liked horror, the questions kept coming up. One of his answers involved social criticism. He referred to increasing problems with inflation, drugs,

Stephen King with his son Joe in 1988. (Courtesy of Getty Images.)

AIDS, sharply rising medical costs, and unemployment. "What you do when you've got a lot of things that you're really afraid of is you sublimate them into something that's not real and you find a place to escape," King said. Another reason people like horror, he said, is because "we've become an increasingly secular society and that means that we don't have the traditional outlets for contemplating our own mortality." Another time he said, "One of the true signs of God's grace on the face of the earth [is] the ability to go on, day after day, to build meaningful lives, to prepare children in the face of all that. . . . You say to yourself, *Okay, let's go see a horror movie and see how bad it can be, and then if I die in bed it won't be so awful.*"

King rendered the trappings and suffocation he felt from his fame in the 1987 novel *Misery*, autobiographical in that it portrayed an author besieged by a fan. The idea for the story came from a dream King had in which a woman said that fan love was the purest love there is. He wondered: what if a writer fell into the clutches of a psychotic fan? In *Misery*, Paul Sheldon, a writer of serial romances, is imprisoned by Annie Wilkes. It is said that King admitted that he himself was terrified by the scene where Annie breaks Sheldon's ankles to keep him from leaving.

Fame certainly had its benefits along with many burdens. Stephen King took all of them in stride. What he took quite seriously was the writer's responsibility to exercise and protect freedom of speech.

SEVEN

Taking a Stand

K ing's brush with school officials who prohibited him from selling his stories on the playground was his first encounter with censorship. However, the issue hit hard when he was filming *Maximum Overdrive* in North Carolina. The state had recently passed a law making pornography illegal, and King saw authorities in local bookstores clamping down on what they considered risqué material.

Upon his return to Maine, King found that the anti-obscenity movement had taken root there as well. Among the groups that supported censorship were the Maine Christian Civic League, Guardians for Education in Maine, the Pro-Life Education Association, the Maine chapter of the Eagle Forum, and the Women's Christian Temperance Union. With slogans like "Do it for the

Children," they were successful in persuading state legislators to introduce a bill making it a "crime to make, sell, give for value, or otherwise promote obscene material in Maine."

No one wanted to support pornography, but no one could answer what pornography was and who would define it. Those who opposed the bill as censorship countered with slogans like "Don't Make Freedom a Dirty Word." Among these groups were the Maine Civil Liberties Union, the Maine chapter of the National Organization of Women, the Maine Teachers' Organization, the Maine Library Association, and magazine and book distributors in the state.

As the campaign for censorship spread into radio, television, newspapers, magazines, and mailings, King joined the debate. He had faced censorship of his own work: *Carrie, 'Salem's Lot, Misery,* and *The Shining* had been banned by various school officials. In a newspaper article, he wrote, "I think the idea of making it a crime to sell obscene material is a bad one, because it takes the responsibility of saying 'no' out of the hands of citizens and puts it into those of the police and courts." The referendum on the bill was defeated on June 10, 1986, by 72 percent of those who voted.

King never forgot that his publisher had required 100,000 words be cut from *The Stand* when it was published in 1978. This was not the result of censorship so much as heavy editing with an eye toward marketability. In 1990, King restored that cut material and added

50,000 more words. Doubleday, the same publisher that had demanded the cutting of the first edition of the book, reissued it with the title *The Stand: Complete and Uncut*. *Publishers Weekly* announced that the added words made the original version even better. Of all King's books, this has been his most popular work.

Because *The Stand* was so popular, TV producers brought it to the screen. The plot was complicated, and the adaptation became an eight-hour miniseries. King wrote the screenplay and was the executive producer. The project featured an all-star cast, including King in a cameo role as a truck driver. The series drew a large, appreciative audience.

King had a new worry. He realized that no editor was likely to criticize his work since his books were so popular. He said, "At this point nobody can make me change anything. . . . That's why it becomes more and more important that I listen carefully to what people say. . . . I have to make those changes even when I don't want to, because it's easy to hang yourself. You get all this freedom—it can lead to self-indulgence."

As he continued to muse about this situation, King decided that he had to move away from writing about Castle Rock, the fictional town which had appeared in so many of his books, although he felt comfortable there. He spoke of authors who wrote constantly about the same locations: "You begin to accept boundaries; the familiarity of the place discourages risks. So I am burning my bridges and destroying the town.

It's all gone—kaput. It's sad but it had to be done."

In a speech at the annual American Booksellers Convention in 1992, King once again denounced censorship. Throughout the years, many well-known books have been banned by various groups claiming that the material is unwholesome for young minds, damaging to developing personalities, or immoral according to the tenets of some religions. Included in this list are "Little Red Riding Hood" (because in some versions the little girl brought wine to her grandmother in her basket), *Charlie and the Chocolate Factory* (because it depicted greedy children), *Where the Wild Things Are* (because it showed a disobedient child), the Harry Potter books (because some groups objected to the inclusion of magic), and books like *Carrie* and *It* (because they featured evil). The list of books notable for both long-standing critical acclaim and that they had at one time been banned is long and includes *The Diary of Anne Frank, The Adventures of Huckleberry Finn, To Kill a Mockingbird,* and several works of William Shakespeare.

As one of the most frequently banned contemporary writers, King had a lot to say on the matter. He quoted from an op-ed piece he had written for a Bangor newspaper after *The Dead Zone* and *The Tommyknockers* were banned from the local school. He advised students, "Hit the public library, read the books, and find out what makes them so horrible that they must be yanked from the school library." He admitted that a fight against censorship would be a never-ending battle, but said that was no reason to accept it without a struggle.

Another issue King wanted to pursue at the convention was the plight of the homeless. Nationwide, many lawmakers had declared that the present welfare system only encouraged dependence on government handouts. There was an increasing push to weed out so-called welfare cheats and a corresponding push to make sure that all people in need received help. An idea that started out as a fund-raising drive to help the homeless revived King's love of playing rock and roll. At the conference, he joined an impromptu band with other writers: humorist Dave Barry; Ridley Pearson, best-selling crime novelist; novelist and nonfiction writer Barbara Kingsolver; and Rev. Robert Fulghum, best known for writing *All I Really Need to Know I Learned in Kindergarten*. The writers named their group the Rock Bottom Remainders for the "remainder books" that a bookseller heavily discounts to liquidate his stock. They hooked up electric guitars and amplifiers at the nearby Cowboy Boogie Bar, and audiences flocked to buy tickets with money that would be donated to charity. King played guitar and, to the delight of the audience, sang "Sea of Love" in an imitation of Bruce Springsteen. Wall to wall, people danced, laughed, and cheered.

The Remainders liked playing together so much they added a saxophone and drums to their group and went on tour. They donated proceeds to several different charities, including Literacy for America and America Scores, a program that combines sports and educational challenges.

King plays the guitar while fellow Rock Bottom Remainders member Amy Tan sings during one of their benefit shows in the 1990s. (Courtesy of AP Photos.)

When he was asked what he thought of America, King had a ready answer. "I think it's fantastic. We're killing ourselves; we're fiddling while Rome burns. I mean, while we've got enough explosives to turn planet Earth into the second asteroid belt, the largest weekly magazine in the country is talking about where celebrities shop, and why people in Hollywood don't want to serve finger foods any more. It all seems really ridiculous to me, but I love it."

In giving back to society, King chose causes and methods that were close to his heart. Having kept his love of baseball—and especially the Boston Red Sox—strong from the years when he was a sportswriter for the *Lisbon Enterprise*, King decided to give something to the game. He said, "Baseball has saved my life. . . . I was a latch-key kid before anyone knew what a latch-key kid was. I would watch baseball when I got home from school. I listened to the games on the radio before that." His son Owen played Little League baseball, and King was a part-time coach and scorekeeper. He donated over

Avid baseball fan Stephen King, with his wife Tabitha to his right, prepares to throw out the first pitch at the Senior League Baseball World Series at Mansfield Stadium in Bangor, Maine. (Courtesy of AP Photos.)

$1 million for the construction of Mansfield Stadium, a state-of-the-art ballpark used by the Little League and Bangor schools. When given an award for community service from the Bangor Chamber of Commerce, King said simply, "We've never said, 'Maybe life would have been better if we had gone to the southern part of the state.' Whatever we've done for Bangor was the result of what Bangor has done for us." The Kings were quiet about their charitable donations, but word did get out quickly when they gave $11.7 million to the public library.

King always kept a local focus on his charitable efforts. He has long been one of the most outspoken advocates for his home state, beginning in the late 1980s when he lobbied hard for the movie adaptation of *Pet Sematary* to be filmed in Maine. The project brought millions of dollars into the local economy. Most recently, King used his 2005 commencement address at his alma mater, the University of Maine, to urge graduates to remain in the state: "Let me tell you a secret: right now you are all sitting on the ground floor of the greatest place on earth, and the elevator doors are open."

King took up the cause of independent booksellers in the fall of 1994 while promoting his 800-page novel *Insomnia*. This is a slow-paced story of an elderly widower who finds himself increasingly unable to sleep more than a few hours each night. Labeling it as a book guaranteed to keep the reader up all night, King toured across the country giving signings only at independent bookstores. He condemned big-box bookstores that offer best sellers at a deep discount, sometimes as much as 40 percent. He said, "It's bad for American thought when American fiction is represented only by Sidney Sheldon, Danielle Steele, Tom Clancy, and Steve King . . . it's a dangerous philosophy."

King was willing to experiment with new modes of marketing. He agreed to write a 30,000-word novel in chapter installments, also known as chapbooks. As a boy, he had loved the installments of the serials in the *Saturday Evening Post*, and now he had an opportunity to hold readers in suspense as he had been held. Each installment had to summarize the previous chapters and include a climax that encouraged the readers to look for the next installment. Writing in installments is risky for

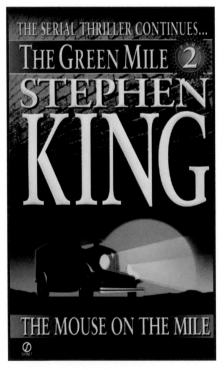

This chapbook was the second of six installments in the series The Green Mile.

a storyteller like King, who lets his characters decide what to do next. As each installment is published, each character becomes indelible in the reader's mind, so King could not go back and change personalities or events. This project became *The Green Mile*, the story of a black convict accused of murdering two white girls and of his relationship with his white jailer. In this work, King raises questions about the existence (or nonexistence) of God and considers the possibility that Jesus Christ has been returning to our world repeatedly for centuries, waiting for us to recognize and embrace him instead of killing him over and over again. Popular from the time of publication, the book took on a new life when it became a movie in which Tom Hanks starred.

One of the most prestigious honors a piece of short fiction can receive is inclusion in *The O. Henry Prize Stories*. In 1996, King took top honors in that publication for "The Man in the Black Suit." King used an old New England storytelling tradition in which a character meets a devil in the woods. In this story he also questions the existence of God, as Gary, the main character, faces death, terrorized by the thought that God may not be in heaven waiting for him. The suspense grows almost unbearable as Gary confronts the fact that he will not know the answer to his question until he is dead.

The O. Henry award marked one of the first times King received official recognition from the literary community. For years, he had racked up awards from various organizations dedicated to genre writing, including the Bram Stoker, the Horror Guild, the Hugo, the Locus, and the World Fantasy awards, several of them many times over. The O. Henry honor marked a shift in how King's work was being perceived and appreciated.

King has said publicly that he would never win a prestigious National Book Award because of prejudice against popular writers and because many people believe that horror is inherently unhealthy and aberrant. He disagrees with that assessment, saying, "The great appeal of horror fiction through the ages is that it serves as a rehearsal for our own deaths." In his writing he moves beyond that fear into complex issues of morality and conscience; love and lust; childhood and adult disillusionment; the existence—or not—of God; euthanasia; abortion; racial tension; spousal abuse. When critics denounce his books as fantasy, he denounces the critics. He says people who don't like fantasy "simply can't lift the weight of fantasy. The muscles of the imagination have grown too weak."

One year, he accepted his invitation to the National Book Award dinner and sat with other popular writers like John Grisham, a best-selling suspense novelist. King and those at his table made it clear that their presence at the dinner was a protest against award committees that refuse to consider all work equally.

In April 1999, a tragedy occurred that forced King to reconsider his own work quite seriously. A school shooting in Columbine, Colorado, shook the nation. King's novel *Rage* depicted events similar to those monopolizing newspaper headlines. King said that he had written many books about teenagers pushed to violent acts, but in *Rage* he came close to giving a blueprint for committing violence. When asked directly if his book had contributed to the killings, he said, "I've spent sleepless nights with the question, and I still don't know. . . . What gives me comfort is the sure knowledge that the book was written with no bad intent." He forbade the publisher to print any more copies of the book.

An interviewer once asked King what he reads when he wants to be frightened. "I think the things that scare me are reading about what's happening to the environment, the destruction of the rain forest. I still wish that I didn't know the statistics about the constant rate at which it's disappearing and what's happening to the atmosphere of the planet as a result. And I think what's worse is this sort of existential comedy of knowing we are demanding these forests to make more cows so McDonald's can make more hamburgers. . . . We're destroying the Earth for Ronald McDonald—think about it. And they say *I* write horror."

Ironically, it was King's love of the outdoors that stirred up a new pot of fears for the writer and presented the greatest challenge he had ever known.

EIGHT

Never Say "The End"

W hen King asked novelist Amy Tan if there was any question she wished a fan would ask, Tan said she wished she were asked about her use of language. This answer inspired King to write a book describing how he became a writer and elaborating on what he knew about the craft of writing and what he could pass along to beginning writers. That idea became *On Writing*. Along with information that was available in other books about writing, King presented his own philosophy. He also challenged the would-be writer: "Some of this book—perhaps too much—has been about how I learned to do it. Much of it has been about how you can do it better. The rest of it—and perhaps the best of it—is a permission slip: you can, you should, and if you're brave enough to start, *you will*. Writing is magic, as much the water of life as any other creative art. The water is free. So drink. Drink and be filled up."

King began writing the book in late 1997, but it didn't come out as smoothly as most of his novels did, and he actually put the book away for a long period of time. In June 1999, reinvigorated after reading what he had put down earlier, he prepared to finish the manuscript.

In order to prepare for his daily writing, King liked to first get a little thinking time. "I just walk around for about four miles, sort of sniffing at this book in my mind." He added, "I don't take notes; I don't outline; I don't do anything like that. I just flail away at the goddamned thing. I start with an idea, and sometimes I even have an idea of where I'm going, but it usually turns out to be someplace else that I end up."

On June 19, a day King will never forget, he went out on his daily four-mile walk on the road near his home in Bangor. Around four o'clock in the afternoon he turned onto the highway at Route 5. He remembers seeing a van coming toward him. His next memory was of lying in a ditch beside the road. His right leg hurt. He wiped blood from his eyes and saw a man sitting on a rock near a van that was parked at the side of the road. This man was Bryan Smith, the driver of the van, and he told King that help was on the way.

King lost consciousness, and when he awoke he saw an ambulance with its lights blazing. An emergency medical technician assured him that he would live, but King needed to get to a hospital fast. At the hospital, doctors determined that they would not be able to treat him, so they put King on a helicopter to send him to a medical center in Lewiston. Upon arrival, he passed in and out of consciousness and was aware only of glimpses of faces, X-ray machines, voices, and hands.

The doctors found that King's lower leg was broken in nine places and his knee was split almost directly down the middle. His hip was fractured, his spine chipped, four ribs were broken, and a laceration in his scalp needed about twenty-five stitches.

After five surgeries, the doctors fit King's leg with steel rods and pins, which had to be removed three times a day so medical personnel could swab out the holes with hydrogen peroxide—an excruciating procedure. A week after King entered the hospital, he took three staggering steps and almost cried with pain and frustration. He went through physical therapy with a walker and slowly learned to take steady steps. About two weeks after entering the hospital, he sat in a wheelchair to watch the Fourth of July fireworks.

After about three weeks, he left the hospital, weighing fifty pounds less than when he entered. He began a daily therapy program of stretching, bending, and trying to walk with a crutch. A month later, he was back in the hospital to have the pins removed so that he could bend his knee. The surgery was successful, and he returned home to his rigid schedule of rehabilitation.

Bryan Smith, while indicted on two felony counts, was allowed by the local district attorney to plead to

Tabitha and Stephen King appear at the premiere of the movie adaptation of The Green Mile *in New York City six months after King's accident.* (Courtesy of Getty Images.)

lesser charges. He served no prison time but died in his small trailer of undetermined causes before his driving rights were returned.

King was still in a lot of pain and worried about becoming addicted to his pain pills after having fought so hard and for so long to stay sober. If ever there was a time that he needed to get back to writing, the endeavor that sustained him, and to understand and rekindle its importance to him, this was the time. He resolved to finish *On Writing* that summer.

Tabby furnished a little space in the back hall with a computer, printer, and the manuscript on which he had been working. She wheeled him into this space and then left him. In his first session there, he spent an hour and forty minutes, the longest time he had sat upright since the accident. His hip and back and leg hurt; sweat dripped off his brow. It was difficult to get back in the rhythm of creating a manuscript again. But at the end of the session he had made a significant step toward returning to writing. He hardly broke his momentum again despite two more operations and some serious infections.

In *On Writing* he answers the questions most frequently asked of him. King recommends that each writer create for himself a state of mind where he shuts himself away from his personal problems. King creates his own mental environment by playing hard rock and roll, which shuts out the rest of the world. He says anyone who has talent and writes for an hour and a half a day for ten years is going to become a good writer. The talent is essential. King offered himself as an example: he has been playing the guitar, with no talent, for almost twenty years, and has barely progressed from the level he attained two years after he began.

Plotting is usually a downfall for a writer, according to King. This is because, he says, our lives are plotless, no matter how much we try to plan them. A story that is tightly plotted will be unreal and lifeless. Instead of a plot, King creates a situation and then asks what if. *'Salem's Lot* asks what if vampires invade a small New England town. *Desperation* wonders what if a policeman goes berserk. *Dolores Claiborne* asks what if a woman is under suspicion for a murder she did not commit. Once his characters face a predicament, King is eager to find out how they react.

Reading *On Writing* is as close as anyone can get to a tutorial from Stephen King, including a dose of the same straight talk he has always favored. He issues a warning with this book. "This is a short book," he says, "because most books about writing are filled with bullshit. Fiction writers, present company included, don't under-stand very much about what they do. . . . I figured the shorter the book, the less the bullshit."

Despite his overwhelming success, King continued to experiment. A year after his accident, he published "Riding the Bullet" over the Internet as an e-book. About 400,000 customers paid to download the story of a college student forced to sacrifice either his own life or

Stephen King appears on the cover of Time *in March 2000 as an emblem of the electronic publishing craze.* (Courtesy of Getty Images.)

DO-IT-YOURSELF .COM If Stephen King can do it, so can you. Who needs Hollywood when you can make your own movies, books and music?

his mother's. With this project, King drew a lot of attention to the electronic publishing issue. Always interested in new territory, King was intrigued by the possibilities—and the pitfalls—electronic publishing offered.

His next venture into online publishing came with a web serialization of *The Plant*, the book he had given to friends and family as a Christmas present almost annually beginning in 1982. King offered the story on the honor system: "You gotta kick a buck; a dollar an episode seems fair enough to me. If it seems fair to you, email the web site and say so . . . honesty is the best policy." Over the course of several months, many people downloaded the material without paying. King pulled it off the Internet.

In 2003, Viking reissued the Dark Tower books, the first of which, *The Gunslinger,* had been published in 1982. Over the next three years, all four of the previously published Dark Tower books saw reissue while three new installments saw publication, culminating in the seventh and final book, known simply as *The Dark Tower*. The vision he had first imagined more than thirty years before was finally complete.

As for his health, King told a reporter in 2003 he was about 75 percent recovered: "I can go out and shoot baskets. I can walk fine, too, though toward the end of the day I pick up a pretty noticeable limp. I still haven't gotten full motion of my right leg, but I'm determined to get it back." Though his recovery was difficult, King had the support of his family. His enormous fame made guarding their privacy a constant battle, but he and Tabby were insistent that their children not live life in the spotlight. Tabby had steadfastly promoted Stephen's career, but once their children were older, she devoted time to publishing several novels of her own.

In November 2003, the National Book Foundation awarded King its medal for Distinguished Contribution to American Letters despite protest from the old guard of the literary community. The National Book Foundation is the same organization that bestows the National Book Award, and is the organization that King had once predicted would never recognize his work. King, who always portrayed himself and many of his characters as an outsider, became a member of a group of "insider" novelists like Toni Morrison, Philip Roth, Ray Bradbury, and, most recently, Judy Blume. The executive director of the foundation, Neil Baldwin, said "Stephen King's

writing is securely rooted in the great American tradition that glorifies spirit-of-place and the abiding power of narrative. He crafts stylish, mind-bending page-turners that contain profound moral truths—some beautiful, some harrowing—about our inner lives."

In his acceptance speech, King spoke to his critics: "We can build bridges between the popular and the literary if we keep our minds and hearts open . . . I hope you all find something good to read tonight or tomorrow . . . something that will fill you up as the evening has filled me up."

King may never gain full admission into the exclusive literary club, but that will by no means diminish his achievements. Strange as it may seem, numbers might do the best job of putting his career in perspective. There are over 300 million copies of his novels, stories, and nonfiction in print in dozens of countries and languages. His novels and stories have been adapted into almost fifty productions, both on television and in movie theaters.

At age fifty-eight, he talks of slowing down even as evidence would indicate otherwise; he recently published a book with author Stewart O'Nan about his beloved Boston Red Sox, and a new crime novel will appear sometime in the fall of 2005. King said, "I'm writing but at a much slower pace than previously and I think that if I come up with something really, really

Opposite: *King accepts the Distinguished Contribution to American Letters Award in November 2003.* (Courtesy of AP Photos.)

good, I would be perfectly willing to publish it because that feels like the final act of the creative process. . . . Writing is still a big, important part of my life and of every day."

In fewer than five decades, King has grown from the little boy who rewrote movies and comic books to the most widely read, most successful writer of the twentieth century. He persevered through the insecurities of adolescence, hundreds of rejections, addiction problems, attempts by critics to label him a hack, an onslaught of would-be book censors, and fans who unceasingly demand attention. The child whose single mother had to move frequently to support her family now generously supports charities ranging in focus from Little League baseball to libraries.

Some people read King for sheer escape, some for the thrill of a scare, some for the themes of good versus evil and insiders versus outsiders, and still others out of love for a great story. For all these readers, the king of horror has a message: "If you don't believe anything else, believe this: when I take you by your hand and begin to talk, my friend, believe every word I say."

TIMELINE

1947	Stephen King is born in Portland, Maine.
1965	Writes first novel-length manuscript, *The Aftermath;* sells first short story, "I Was a Teenage Grave Robber," to *Comics Review*.
1966	Enrolls at the University of Maine in Orono.
1970	Graduates from the University of Maine.
1971	Marries Tabitha Spruce; daughter Naomi is born; begins teaching at Hampden Academy.
1972	Son Joseph is born.
1973	Sells first novel, *Carrie,* for $2,500; subsequently sells paperback rights for $400,000.
1977	Son Owen is born.
1981	Receives Career Alumni Award from the University of Maine.
1982	Plays supporting role in *Creepshow*.
1985	Admits he wrote under pseudonym Richard Bachman; writes and directs screenplay *Maximum Overdrive*.
1990	Performs with Rock Bottom Remainders for the first time.
1996	Gains entry into the *Guinness Book of World Records* for having six books on the bestseller list at one time.
1999	Nearly killed when a drunk driver runs him over on a country road in Maine.
2003	Awarded 2003 Medal for Distinguished Contribution to American Letters by the National Book Foundation.

Major works

1974	*Carrie*
1975	*'Salem's Lot*
1977	*The Shining, Rage* (as Richard Bachman)
1978	*The Stand, Night Shift,*
1979	*The Dead Zone, The Long Walk* (as Richard Bachman)
1980	*Firestarter*
1981	*Danse Macabre, Cujo, Roadwork* (as Richard Bachman)
1982	*Different Seasons, The Dark Tower: The Gunslinger, Creepshow, The Running Man* (as Richard Bachman)
1983	*Christine, Pet Sematary, Cycle of the Werewolf*
1984	*The Talisman* (with Peter Straub), *Thinner* (as Richard Bachman)
1985	*Skeleton Crew, The Bachman Books* (reissue of previously published books)
1986	*It*
1987	*Misery, The Eyes of the Dragon, The Tommyknockers, The Dark Tower II: The Drawing of the Three*
1989	*The Dark Half*
1990	*The Stand: Complete and Uncut, Four Past Midnight*
1991	*Needful Things, The Dark Tower III: The Waste Lands*
1992	*Gerald's Game*
1993	*Nightmares & Dreamscapes, Dolores Claiborne*
1994	*Insomnia*
1995	*Rose Madder*
1996	*Desperation, The Green Mile* (serial novel), *The Regulators*
1997	*The Dark Tower IV: Wizard and Glass, Six Stories*
1998	*Bag of Bones*
1999	*Storm of the Century, The Girl Who Loved Tom Gordon, Hearts in Atlantis*
2000	*On Writing: A Memoir of the Craft*

2001	*Black House* (with Peter Straub), *Dreamcatcher*
2002	*Everything's Eventual*
2003	*From a Buick 8, The Dark Tower V: Wolves of the Calla*
2004	*The Dark Tower VI: Song of Susannah, The Dark Tower VII: The Dark Tower, Faithful* (with Stewart O'Nan)

Major awards

1980	Writer of the Year from *People* magazine
1981	Career Alumni Award from the University of Maine, Nebula Award for "The Way Station"
1982	British Fantasy Award for "Do the Dead Sing?", Hugo Award for *Danse Macabre,* Locus Award for *Danse Macabre*
1986	Locus Award for *Skeleton Crew*
1987	Bram Stoker Award for *Misery*
1990	Bram Stoker Award for *Four Past Midnight*
1995	Bram Stoker Award for "Lunch at the Gotham Café," World Fantasy Award for "The Man in the Black Suit"
1996	Bram Stoker Award for *The Green Mile,* O. Henry Award for "The Man in the Black Suit"
1997	Horror Guild Award for *Desperation,* Locus Award for *Desperation*
1998	Bram Stoker Award for *Bag of Bones*
1999	Locus Award for *Bag of Bones*
2000	Bram Stoker Award for *On Writing*
2001	Horror Guild Award for *On Writing*
2002	Horror Guild Award for *Black House*
2003	Horror Guild Awards for *From a Buick 8* and *Everything's Eventual,* Horror Writers' Association Lifetime Achievement Award, National Book Foundation medal for Distinguished Contribution to American Letters
2004	Lifetime achievement award from the World Fantasy convention.

SOURCES

CHAPTER ONE: Learning Fear

p. 9, "I'm going to go out . . ." A & E video, *Stephen King: Fear, Fame and Fortune* (New York: New Video 2001).

p. 12, "He splattered. . . ." King, *On Writing : A Memoir of the Craft* (New York: Charles Scribners' Sons, 2000), 23.

p. 13, "I didn't sleep . . ." Stephen King, *Danse Macabre* (New York: Berkley Books, 1981), 118.

p. 13, "Relax, Stevie . . ." King, *On Writing,* 24.

p. 13, "should be jailed immediately . . ." Ibid., 25.

p. 13, "I think that . . ." Ibid.

p. 15, "cheap vacations," George Beahm, *The Stephen King Story: A Literary Profile* (Kansas City: Andrews and McMeel, 1991), 16.

p. 18, "I wanna do that . . ." Underwood, *Feast of Fear,* 25.

CHAPTER TWO: Writer Rebel

p. 24-25, "I'd meet [the postman] . . ." Stephen King, *Different Seasons* (New York: The Viking Press, 1982), 509.

p. 28, "In an odd way . . ." John Wukovits, *Stephen King* (San Diego, CA: Lucent Books, 1999), 25.

p. 29, "John Gould taught . . ." *On Writing,* 46.

p. 30, "an extraordinary book . . ." Beahm, *The Stephen King Story,* 8-9.

p. 30, "big goofy kid . . ." A & E Video.

p. 30, "I could write . . ." Beahm, *The Stephen King Story,* 121.

p. 31, "For me, rock 'n roll . . ." Underwood, *Feast of Fear,* 61.

CHAPTER THREE: The Art of Persistence

p. 33, "There's a constant fear . . ." George Beahm, *Stephen*

King: America's Best-loved Boogeyman (Kansas City, MO: Andrews McMeel Publishing, 1998), 12.

p. 35, "A huge white maggot . . ." Ibid., 10.

p. 38, "It's a novel . . ." Beahm, *The Stephen King Story,* 29.

p. 40, "When I was . . ." Ibid., 46.

p. 41, "couldn't even like . . ." Beahm, *Boogeyman,* 17.

p. 43, "good saints, how I feared . . ." Robert Browning, *Selected Poetry of Robert Browning* (New York: The Modern Library, 1951), 282.

p. 44, "like a millworker . . ." King, *On Writing,* 51.

p. 44, "Everything funny is horrible . . ." Underwood, *Feast,* 132.

p. 45, "If you visualize . . ." Ibid., 16.

p. 45, "Steve would come in . . ." Wukovits, *Stephen King,* 31.

p. 46, "Can you imagine . . ." Beahm, *Boogeyman,* 46.

p. 46, "The man in the black suit fled . . ." Stephen King, *The Dark Tower: The Gunslinger* (New York: New American Library, 1982), 11.

CHAPTER FOUR: The Success of Horror

p. 50, "The real impetus . . ." Beahm, *The Stephen King Story,* 53.

p. 52, "There I was, unpublished . . ." Wukovits, *Stephen King,* 37.

p. 54, "bogus documentation . . ." Beahm, *The Stephen King Story,* 59

p. 54, "almost immediately struck drunk," Ibid., 60.

p. 55, "CONGRATULATIONS, CARRIE OFFICIALLY . . ." King, *On Writing,* 83.

p. 57, "a contender for the bloodiest . . ." Beahm, *The Stephen King Story,* 66.

p. 57, "Good, bad, or indifferent . . ." Beahm, *Boogeyman,* 30.

p. 57, "I think I did . . ." King, *On Writing,* 94.

p. 58-59, "On the one hand . . ." Beahm, *Boogeyman,* 39.

p. 60, "The first time I realized . . ." Beahm, *The Stephen King Story,* 70.

p. 60-61, "First the telekinetic . . . just fine," *Stephen King, Different Seasons,* (New York: Viking Press, 1982), 501.

p. 61, "That's OK, Bill . . ." Ibid.

p. 62, "No, that's not me . . ." Underwood, *Feast,* 46

p. 62, "what Stephen King would write . . ." Stephen Spignesi, *The Essential Stephen King* (Franklin Lakes, NJ: New Page Books, 2001), 158.

CHAPTER FIVE: Terrorizing the Reader . . . and Writer

p. 64, "I don't really do anything . . ." Underwood, *Feast,* 255.

p. 65, "Wanted: a draughty Victorian . . ." Beahm, *The Stephen King Story,* 80.

p. 66, "the thought of having . . ." King, *Danse Macabre,* xvii.

p. 67, "Maybe there will be . . ." Ibid.

p. 67, "I recognize terror . . ." Spignesi, *The Essential Stephen King,* 85.

p. 67, "The good horror tale . . ." King, *Danse Macabre,* 4.

p. 67, "*Danse Macabre* is a conversation . . ." King, *Danse Macabre,* opening page.

p. 68-69, "Now, there are lots . . ." Stephen King, "National Book Awards 2003," National Book Foundation, http://www.nationalbook.org/nbaacceptspeech_sking.html (accessed June 20, 2005).

p. 70, "Death is it. . . ." Beahm, *The Stephen King Story,* 84-85.

p. 70, "worst-case analysis," Ibid., 85.

p. 70, "The last 50 pages . . ." Beahm, *Boogeyman,* 84.

p. 73, "That's not negotiable . . ." Underwood, *Feast,* 102.

p. 76, "I certainly didn't find . . ." Spignesi, *The Essential Stephen King,* 117.

p. 76, "Sooner or later . . ." King, *Different Seasons,* 501-2.

p. 77, "When I worked on my half . . ." Spignesi, *The Essential Stephen King,* 58.

CHAPTER SIX: Bestsellasaurus Rex

p. 81, "I thought it was time . . ." Spignesi, *The Essential Stephen King,* 126.

p. 81, "It's like this great big . . ." Beahm, *Boogeyman,* 61.

p. 82, "I would leave . . ." Underwood, *Feast,* 183.

p. 83, "This guy comes in . . ." Ibid., 211.

p. 83-84, "not under any circumstances . . ." Ibid., 262.

p. 84, "In horror fiction . . ." Beahm, *The Stephen King Story,* 118.

p. 84-85, "When I'm not recognized . . ." Ibid., 105.

p. 85, "That's just what paranoid people . . ." Underwood, *Feast,* 51.

p. 86, "I hate Halloween . . ." Ibid, 79.

p. 86, "I was pissed . . ." Beahm, *Boogeyman,* 99.

p. 86, "cancer of the pseudonym" Ibid., 133.

p. 87, "Bestsellasaurus Rex . . ." Ibid., 85.

p. 88, "I was halfway down . . ." Stephen King, *Skeleton Crew* (New York: G. P. Putnam's Sons, 1985), Notes.

p. 90, "To keep you up-to-date . . ." Beahm, *Boogeyman,* 97.

p. 91, "What you do when . . ." Underwood, *Feast,* 231.

p. 91, "we've become an increasingly . . ." Ibid.

p. 91, "One of the true signs . . ." Beahm, *Boogeyman,* 55.

CHAPTER SEVEN: Taking a Stand

p. 93, "crime to make . . ." Beahm, *Boogeyman,* 105.

p. 93, "I think the idea . . ." Ibid.,106.

p. 94, "At this point . . ." Ibid., 122.

p. 94-95, "You begin to accept . . ." Ibid., 141.

p. 95, "Hit the public library . . ." Ibid., 172.

p. 97-98, "I think it's fantastic . . ." Underwood, *Feast,* 111.

p. 98, "Baseball has saved . . ." Beahm, Boogeyman, 174.

p. 99, "We've never said . . ." Ibid., 177.

p. 99, "Let me tell you . . ." http://www.stephenking.com/com_address/

p. 100, "It's bad for American thought . . ." Beahm, *Boogeyman,* 182.

p. 102, "The great appeal . . ." Wukovits, *Stephen King,* 178.

p. 102, "simply can't lift . . ." King, *Danse Macabre,* 99.

p. 103, "I've spent sleepless nights . . ." Stephen King, "The Importance of Being Bachman," Unofficial Stephen King, http://stephenking.kraftyworld.co.uk/rb.htm (accessed August 12, 2005).

p. 103, "I think the things . . ." Beahm, *The Stephen King Story,* 168-169.

CHAPTER EIGHT: Never Say "The End"

p. 104-105, "Some of this book . . ." King, *On Writing,* 270.

p. 105, "I just walk around . . ." Underwood, *Feast,* 218.

p. 105, "I don't take notes . . ." Ibid., 267.

p. 109, "This is a short book . . ." King, *On Writing,* 11.

p. 110, "You gotta kick a buck . . ." Spignesi, *The Essential Stephen King,* 177.

p. 111, "I can go out . . ." Joseph P. Kahn, "Into the Woods with Stephen King," *Boston Sunday Globe,* March 16, 2003, N10.

p. 111,113, "Stephen King's writing . . ." Press Release, National Book Foundation, http://www.nationalbook.org/dcal_2003.html (accessed June 20, 2005).

p. 113, "We can build bridges . . ." http://www.nationalbook.org/nbaacceptspeech_sking.html

p. 113-114, "I'm writing, but . . ." Stephen King, "Frequently Asked Questions," Stephen King.com: The Official Web Site, http://www.stephenking.com/pages/FAQ/Stephen_King/retired.php

p. 114, "If you don't believe . . ." Beahm, *The Stephen King Story,* 181.

BIBLIOGRAPHY

Beahm, George. *Stephen King: America's Best-Loved Boogeyman.* Kansas City: Andrews McMeel Publishing, 1998.

Beahm, George. *The Stephen King Story: A Literary Profile.* Kansas City: Andrews and McMeel, 1991.

Boston Sunday Globe, March 16, 2003.

Browning, Robert. *Selected Poetry of Robert Browning.* New York: The Modern Library, 1951.

Collings, Michael. *The Many Facets of Stephen King.* Washington: Starmont House, Inc., 1985.

Coddon, Karin, ed. *Readings on Stephen King.* San Diego,CA: Greenhaven Press, 2004.

Kahn, Joseph P. "Into the Woods with Stephen King." *Boston Globe,* March 16, 2003, sec. N.

King, Stephen. *The Bachman Books.* New York: New American Library, 1985.

———. *Danse Macabre.* New York: Berkley Books, 1981.

———. *Different Seasons.* New York: Viking Press, 1982.

———. *The Gunslinger.* New York: New American Library, 1982.

———. "The Importance of Being Bachman." Unofficial Stephen King. http://stephenking.kraftyworld.co.uk/rb.htm.

———. *It.* New York: New American Library, 1987.

———. *On Writing: A Memoir of the Craft*. New York: Charles Scribner's Sons, 2000.

———. *Skeleton Crew*. New York: G. P. Putnam's Sons, 1985.

Spignesi, Stephen. *The Essential Stephen King*. New Jersey: New Page Books, 2001.

Stephen King: Fear, Fame, and Fortune. A & E Video, 2001.

Underwood, Tim and Chuck Miller, eds. *Feast of Fear: Conversations with Stephen King*. New York: Carroll & Graf Publishers, Inc. 1989.

Wiater, Stanley, Christopher Golden, and Hank Wagner. *The Stephen King Universe*. Los Angeles: Renaissance Books, 2001.

Wukovits, John. *Stephen King*. San Diego: Lucent Books, 1999.

WEB SITES

http://www.stephenking.com
The official, authorized Stephen King site contains an exhaustive list of published works, film and television adaptations, awards, news, information on forthcoming works, and frequently asked questions.

http://www.nationalbook.org/nbaacceptspeech_sking.html
The official Web site of the National Book Foundation includes King's acceptance speech plus information about other annual and lifetime achievement award winners, and the various programs the foundation sponsors.

http://www.horror.org/
The official Web site of the Horror Writers Association lists its winners of the Bram Stoker awards, provides free book excerpts, links to other horror writing-related sites, and a reading list.

INDEX